海外视角汉语教材
A Chinese Textbook from Overseas Perspectives

汉语拼音入门
Hànyǔ   Pīnyīn   Rùmén

Introduction to Standard Chinese *Pinyin* System

编著：
Helen H. Shen
Chen-Hui Tsai   Yunong Zhou

北京语言大学出版社
BEIJING LANGUAGE AND CULTURE
UNIVERSITY PRESS

（京）新登字 157 号

图书在版编目（CIP）数据

汉语拼音入门 ［美］Helen H. Shen（沈禾玲），
　［美］Chen-Hui Tsai（蔡真慧），Yunong Zhou（周虞农）编著.
—北京：北京语言大学出版社，2007
ISBN 978 – 7 – 5619 – 1618 – 6

Ⅰ. 汉…
Ⅱ.①沈…②蔡…③周…
Ⅲ. 汉语拼音 – 对外汉语教学 – 教材
Ⅳ. H195.4

中国版本图书馆 CIP 数据核字（2006）第 054619 号

书　　名：	汉语拼音入门	
中文编辑：	王　轩　周婉梅	
英文编辑：	武思敏	
装帧设计：	苏芳蕾	
责任印制：	汪学发	

出版发行：**北京语言大学出版社**
社　　址：北京市海淀区学院路 15 号　邮政编码 100083
网　　址：www.blcup.com
电　　话：发行部　82303650/3591/3651
　　　　　编辑部　82303647
　　　　　读者服务部　82303653/3908
印　　刷：北京新丰印刷厂
经　　销：全国新华书店

版　　次：2006 年 6 月第 1 版　2007 年 2 月第 2 次印刷
开　　本：889 毫米×1194 毫米　1/16　印张：课本 8.75　练习册 5
字　　数：课本：180 千字　练习册：72 千字　印数：1 – 3000 册
书　　号：ISBN 978 – 7 – 5619 – 1618 – 6/H·06065
定　　价：52.00 元（含课本及录音 CD、练习册及录音 MP3）

凡有印装质量问题，本社负责调换。电话：82303590

目 录

Contents

表和图

Tables and Figures

前　言

　　中国有 13 亿人口，56 个民族。汉族是 56 个民族中人数最多的民族，占中国总人口的
90％。汉族使用的语言称为汉语。现代汉语可分为七大方言，它们与普通话的书写形式是统一
的，但是语音特征稍有不同。这七大方言分别是：北方方言、吴方言、粤方言、湘方言、闽方
言、客家方言和赣方言。北方方言分布在中国的中原、东北、西北及西南地区；吴方言分布在
上海、江苏、浙江一带；粤方言也就是广东话，主要分布在广东和广西两省，香港、澳门地区
也使用粤方言作为主要交际工具；湘方言主要分布在湖南省；闽方言分布在福建、海南、广东
东部、浙江南部及台湾；客家方言也叫客家话，主要分布在广东东部、福建西部、江西南部及
广西东南部；赣方言分布在江西省大部分地区。图 1（见第 5 页）标出了七大方言的分布情
况。七大方言中，说北方方言的人口占汉族人口的 71％（黄伯荣、廖序东）。除了汉族之外，
约 10％ 的中国人是少数民族，他们说各自的语言。

　　现代汉民族共同语（普通话）虽然是以北方方言为基础，以北京语音为标准音，但是也吸
收了许多其他方言的一些表达法，剔除了一些北京话。比如说，普通话并不使用很多儿化音，
所以，普通话不等于北京话。

　　因为用来记录汉语的汉字最初是象形文字，它没有直接的音—形之间的联系。在历史上，
曾使用过不同的语音符号体系来给汉字注音。其中一种叫直音法，这种方法是用一个字来注一
个同音的汉字。反切法是另一种注音方法，这种方法是用两个汉字给一个汉字注音，即用第一
个汉字的声母和第二个汉字的韵母和声调来注另一个汉字的音。后来又用了注音符号，这种方
法是用一套符号系统（简化的古汉字）来代表汉语中不同的音，上个世纪 50 年代之前一段时

间曾在中国大陆使用，现仍然在中国台湾地区使用。汉语拼音（简称拼音）是中国大陆自上个世纪50年代以来一直在使用的汉语语音符号。为了学习汉语普通话，我们得先学汉语语音符号，这本教材的目的就是向初学者介绍汉语普通话的语音符号，也就是拼音。

　　这本教材共有十课。第一课概括地介绍了普通话的发音系统，使大家对这个系统有一个总体的了解。第二至第九课具体介绍如何发每一个音，学习21个声母和36个韵母。除了第二课以外，每课课文大致有三个部分。第一部分介绍拼音符号和每个音的发音方法，在可能的情况下，标出与这个音近似的英语音，并指出它们之间的细微差别；第二部分是课内练习，包括一系列的声、调辨认、区别和发音练习；第三部分是绕口令或诗歌，让学习者在有意义的情境中对学到的拼音进行再练习。第十课对汉语音节的拼写规则和汉语语音的变调规则作一个初步的介绍。教材的最后附有课堂教学常用语，便于学习者使用。除了课本以外，我们还提供相应的课外练习册，可以让学习者在课外进行更多的拼音练习。课本和练习册均配有光盘，方便学习者反复练习。

Introduction

The People's Republic of China has a population of 1. 3 billion which is made up of fifty-six ethnic groups. Han is the largest nationality among these ethnic groups and accounts for 90 percent of the Chinese population. The native language that the Han people speak is called *Hanyu* (the Chinese language). *Hanyu* can be divided into seven major dialects, which share the same written form as *putonghua* while having slightly different phonological properties. The seven major dialects include *mandarin*, *wu*, *yue*,· *xiang*, *min*, *kejia*, and *gan*. *Mandarin* is spoken by Han people in the Central Plains, northeast, northwest and southwest of China. *Wu* dialect is spoken in Shanghai, Jiangsu and Zhejiang. *Yue*, which is also called *Cantonese*, is spoken by the Han population distributed primarily in Guangdong and Guangxi provinces. *Cantonese* is also a major language for communication in Hong Kong and Macao. *Xiang* is mainly spoken by Han people in Hunan province. *Min* dialect is spoken in the areas of Fujian, the east of Guangdong, Hainan, Taiwan and the south of Zhejiang. *Kejia*, known as *Hakkas*, is spoken by Han people in the east of Guangdong, west of Fujian, south of Jiangxi, as well as southeast of Guangxi. And *gan* is spoken in the most parts of Jiangxi province. Among the seven major dialects, *mandarin* is spoken by about 71 percent of the Han population (Huang & Liao 1981). Figure 1 (see page 5) illustrates the geographical distribution of the seven major dialects. In addition to Han nationality, various minority languages are spoken by 10 percent of Chinese people who are minorities.

Standard Chinese is based on *mandarin* and takes Beijing speech sound as the standard pronunciation. However, the standard Chinese has also included many expressions from other dialects and excluded some local colloquial expressions in Beijing dialect. To give one example, standard Chinese uses much less of the [r] retroflexion than the Beijing dialect does. Thus, standard Chinese is not the same as the Beijing dialect.

Since the original Chinese characters were pictographs, they lack sound-to-script correspondence. In earlier times, different phonetic pronunciation systems were used to mark the Chinese characters.

One of the systems is called *Zhiyin* , which provides the pronunciation of a Chinese character by citing another character with the same pronunciation. *Fanqie* is another method which indicates the pronunciation of a new Chinese character by using two other known Chinese characters, the first having the same initial consonant as the given character and the second having the same vowel and tone of the given character. *Zhuyin fuhao* (national phonetic alphabet) is a set of symbols (simplified classical Chinese characters) used to transcribe the pronunciation of characters. It was used in the mainland before the 1950s and is still being used in China's Taiwan province. *Hanyu pinyin* (Chinese Phonetic Alphabet, or *Pinyin* for short) is the phonetic system adopted by the People's Republic of China since the 1950s. In order to learn standard Chinese, one must learn its phonetic system first. The purpose of this textbook is to introduce *Pinyin*, the phonetic alphabet of standard Chinese to the beginners.

This textbook consists of ten lessons. Lesson 1 provides a brief introduction to the standard Chinese phonetic system. Lessons 2 to 9 are designed to teach you how to pronounce each sound through the learning of the *Pinyin* system — 21 initial consonants and 36 simple or compound vowels. Each lesson (except Lesson 2) consists of three sections. Section 1 introduces the phonetic symbols and their ways of pronunciation. And it compares the similarities and differences between Chinese and English in pronouncing a particular sound when it becomes relevant. Section 2 presents classroom exercises including a series of pronunciation activities such as sound and tone recognition, discrimination and pronunciation practice. Section 3 provides exercises such as Chinese tongue twisters or poems for further practicing the introduced sounds in meaningful contexts. Lesson 10 gives a brief introduction of the phonetic spelling rules for writing Chinese syllables and tone changes in the context of intonation patterns. The last part of the textbook, an Appendix, introduces classroom expressions which is helpful to learners for class practice. In addition to the textbook, a workbook provides after-class exercises for each lesson. Both the textbook and the workbook are accompanied by a CD, to enable learners to practice repeatedly.

图1 汉语七大方言地理分布图
Figure 1.　Geographical Distribution of the Seven Major Han Dialects

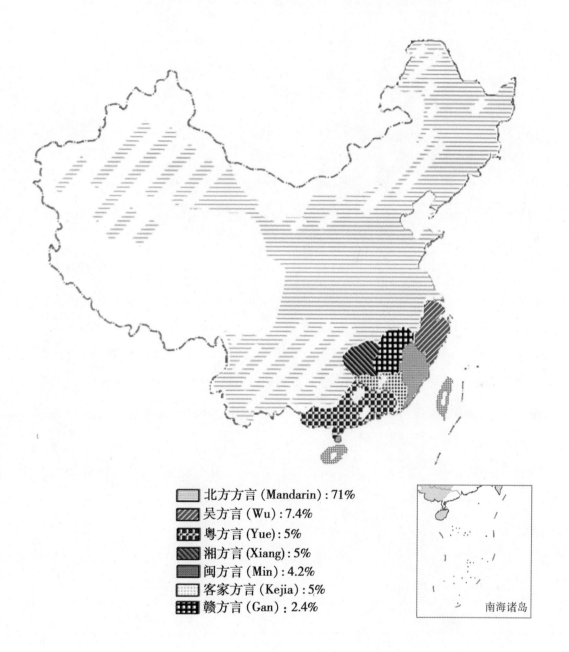

北方方言 (Mandarin) : 71%

吴方言 (Wu) : 7.4%

粤方言 (Yue) : 5%

湘方言 (Xiang) : 5%

闽方言 (Min) : 4.2%

客家方言 (Kejia) : 5%

赣方言 (Gan) : 2.4%

南海诸岛

āéīòu

1

汉语拼音

Chinese *Pinyin*

第一课 汉语拼音

Ⅰ. 汉语拼音简介

汉语拼音使用罗马字母作为书写形式，但两者在发音上却并不相同。见表1：

表1　汉语拼音字母表

Aa	Bb	Cc	Dd	Ee	Ff	Gg	Hh	Ii
ㄚ*	ㄅㄝ	ㄘㄝ	ㄉㄝ	ㄜ	ㄝㄈ	ㄍㄝ	ㄏㄚ	ㄧ
Jj	Kk	Ll	Mm	Nn	Oo	Pp	Qq	Rr
ㄐㄝ	ㄎㄝ	ㄝㄌ	ㄝㄇ	ㄋㄝ	ㄛ	ㄆㄝ	ㄑㄧㄡ	ㄚㄦ
Ss	Tt	Uu	Vv**	Ww	Xx	Yy	Zz	
ㄝㄙ	ㄊㄝ	ㄨ	ㄞㄝ	ㄨㄚ	ㄒㄧ	ㄧㄚ	ㄗㄝ	

*　注音符号（中国台湾地区现仍使用注音符号）

**　根据中国文字改革委员会在 1958 年 2 月发布的《汉语拼音方案》，"v"只用于拼写外来语、
　　少数民族语言和方言。

在介绍汉语音节之前，我们先就汉语语音发音部位的名称作一个整体的介绍，图 1 详细列
出了汉语发音部位的名称及其相对应的位置。

汉语的音节由声母、韵母、声调三个要素组成。声母是音节开头的辅音，韵母是音节中声
母后面的部分，有些音节是没有声母的。汉语普通话一共有 21 个声母（见表 2）和 36 个韵母
（见表 3），36 个韵母当中包含了 7 个单韵母、29 个复韵母，复韵母可进一步细分为复元音韵
母、前鼻韵母及后鼻韵母。

Lesson 1 Chinese Pinyin

I. An overview of Chinese *Pinyin*

Chinese *Pinyin* uses Roman alphabetical letters as its written form but having different pronunciation which is illustrated in Table 1 below:

Table 1. Chinese Phonetic Alphabet

Aa ㄚ*	Bb ㄅㄝ	Cc ㄘㄝ	Dd ㄉㄝ	Ee ㄜ	Ff ㄝㄈ	Gg ㄍㄝ	Hh ㄏㄚ	Ii ㄧ
Jj ㄐㄧㄝ	Kk ㄎㄝ	Ll ㄝㄌ	Mm ㄝㄇ	Nn ㄋㄝ	Oo ㄛ	Pp ㄆㄝ	Qq ㄑㄧㄡ	Rr ㄚㄦ
Ss ㄝㄙ	Tt ㄊㄝ	Uu ㄨ	Vv** ㄪㄝ	Ww ㄨㄚ	Xx ㄒㄧ	Yy ㄧㄚ	Zz ㄗㄝ	

* National phonetic alphabet is still being used in China's Taiwan Province.

* * According to the *Hanyu Pinyin Fang'an* (Scheme for the Chinese Phonetic Alphabet) issued by the Chinese Language Reform Committee (February 1958), "v" is used only to spell foreign languages, languages of national minorities and dialects.

Before introducing Chinese syllables, we need to know the names of the articulators – the parts of the human speech organs used to produce a specific sound. The major articulators involved in pronouncing *Pinyin* are illustrated in Figure 1.

A Chinese syllable usually consists of three elements: the initial consonant, the simple or compound vowel, and the tone. The initial consonant refers to the consonant which appears in the initial position of a syllable, and the simple or compound vowel comes after it. Some syllables can stand alone without initial consonants. There are a total of 21 initial consonants (see Table 2) and 36 simple or compound vowels (see Table 3), which include seven simple vowels and twenty-nine complex vowels-compounds. The complex vowels-compounds can be further divided into three categories: compound vowels, front nasal simple or compound vowels and back nasal simple or compound vowels.

图1　发音部位图

1. 上唇
2. 下唇
3. 上齿
4. 下齿
5. 上齿龈
6. 下齿龈
7. 硬腭
8. 软腭
9. 口腔
10. 鼻腔
11. 舌尖
12. 舌根
13. 声带

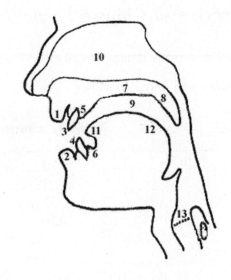

表2　声母表

b	p	m	f	d	t	n	l
ㄅ	ㄆ	ㄇ	ㄈ	ㄉ	ㄊ	ㄋ	ㄌ
g	k	h			j	q	x
ㄍ	ㄎ	ㄏ			ㄐ	ㄑ	ㄒ
zh	ch	sh	r	z	c	s	
ㄓ	ㄔ	ㄕ	ㄖ	ㄗ	ㄘ	ㄙ	

　　声母皆为辅音，韵母则主要由元音构成（有鼻音 n 或 ng 的鼻韵母除外）。辅音与元音最主要的区别在于，发辅音时，呼出的气流在口腔或鼻腔内会受到不同发音部位的阻碍；而发元音时，气流在口腔内通畅无阻。我们会在后面的课文中进一步讲述每个元音和辅音的发音特点。

Figure 1. Points of Articulation

1. Upper lip
2. Lower lip
3. Upper teeth
4. Lower teeth
5. Upper gum
6. Lower gum
7. Hard palate
8. Soft palate
9. Oral cavity
10. Nasal cavity
11. Tip of the tongue
12. Root of the tongue
13. Vocal cords

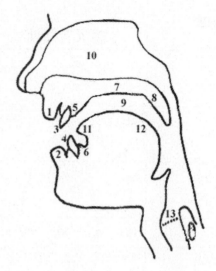

Table 2. Initial Consonants

b	p	m	f	d	t	n	l
ㄅ	ㄆ	ㄇ	ㄈ	ㄉ	ㄊ	ㄋ	ㄌ
g	k	h		j	q	x	
ㄍ	ㄎ	ㄏ		ㄐ	ㄑ	ㄒ	
zh	ch	sh	r	z	c	s	
ㄓ	ㄔ	ㄕ	ㄖ	ㄗ	ㄘ	ㄙ	

Initial consonants are all consonants, while the simple or compound vowels are all vowels except for the vowels followed by the nasal sound "n" or "ng". The major difference in pronouncing consonants and vowels is that when pronouncing a consonant, the air exhaled by our lungs is blocked by one or more of our articulators in either the oral or nasal cavity; while the air flows smoothly without hindrance when pronouncing a vowel. Further details of phonetic features of each vowel and consonant will be discussed in subsequent lessons.

表3　韵母表

单韵母	复韵母		
	复元音韵母	前鼻韵母	后鼻韵母
a ㄚ	ai　ao ㄞ　ㄠ	an ㄢ	ang ㄤ
o ㄛ	ou ㄡ		ong ㄨㄥ
e ㄜ	ei ㄟ	en ㄣ	eng ㄥ
i ㄧ	ia　ie　iao　iou(iu) ㄧㄚ　ㄧㄝ　ㄧㄠ　ㄧㄡ	in　ian ㄧㄣ　ㄧㄢ	iang　ing　iong ㄧㄤ　ㄧㄥ　ㄩㄥ
u ㄨ	ua　uo　uai　uei(ui) ㄨㄚ　ㄨㄛ　ㄨㄞ　ㄨㄟ	uan　uen(un) ㄨㄢ　ㄨㄣ	uang　ueng ㄨㄤ　ㄨㄥ
ü ㄩ	üe ㄩㄝ	üan　ün ㄩㄢ　ㄩㄣ	
er ㄦ			

　　现代汉语普通话有四个基本声调。汉语的每一个音节都有它固定的声调，不同的声调，构成不同的音节，表达不同的意义。我们会在第五课中进一步讨论汉语普通话的四个声调。

Ⅱ. 元音发音规则

　　不同的元音主要是由舌位的高低、前后和嘴唇的圆展决定的，因此，元音可依据下面三项标准来分类：唇形、舌位的垂直位置（高或低）以及舌位的水平位置（前或后）。

Table 3.　Simple or Compound Vowels

Simple vowels	Complex vowels-compounds		
	compound vowels	front nasal simple or compound vowels	back nasal simple or compound vowels
a Y	ai　ao 历　幺	an 弓	ang 尢
o ㄛ	ou 又		ong ㄨㄥ
e ㄜ	ei 乀	en ㄣ	eng ㄥ
i 丨	ia　ie　iao　iou(iu) 丨Y　丨ㄝ　丨幺　丨又	in　ian 丨ㄣ　丨弓	iang　ing　iong 丨尢　丨ㄥ　ㄩㄥ
u ㄨ	ua　uo　uai　uei(ui) ㄨY　ㄨㄛ　ㄨ历　ㄨ乀	uan　uen(un) ㄨ弓　ㄨㄣ	uang　ueng ㄨ尢　ㄨㄥ
ü ㄩ	üe ㄩㄝ	üan　ün ㄩ弓　ㄩㄣ	
er ㄦ			

Every syllable in Chinese has a fixed tone. Four basic tones are used in standard Chinese. In spoken Chinese, a change in tone will bring about a change in the meaning denoted by that syllable. We will discuss the pronunciation of the four tones in detail in Lesson 5.

II.　How to pronounce vowels

The pronunciation of vowels is basically determined by the position of the tongue and the shape of the mouth. Thus vowels can be categorized according to the shapes of the mouth (lips), the vertical positions of the tongue (high vs. low), and the horizontal positions of the tongue (front vs. back).

唇形可区分为圆唇和不圆唇，图示如下：

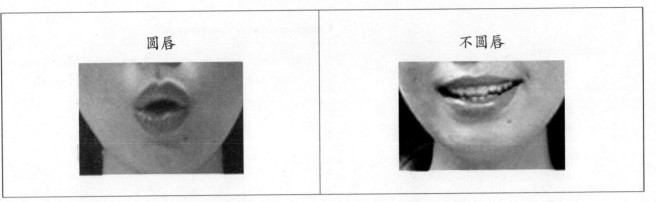

舌位的垂直位置是指发元音时舌头在口腔上端与下端之间的位置，图示如下：

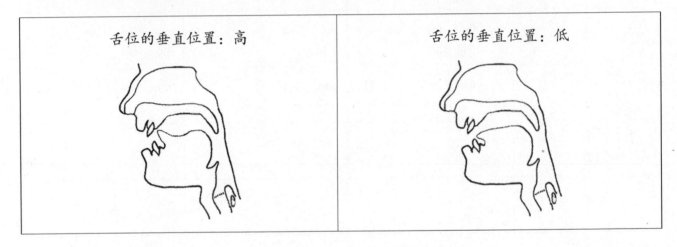

舌位的水平位置是指发元音时舌头的前（靠近牙齿）后（靠近咽喉）位置，图示如下：

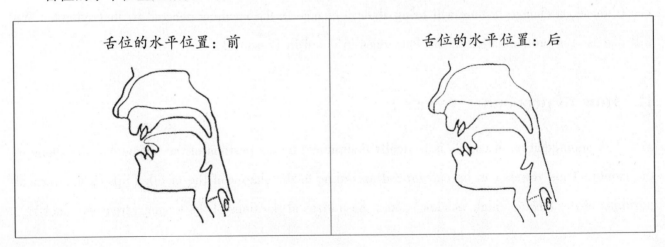

The shape of the mouth（lips）can be divided into two kinds, rounded and unrounded as shown below:

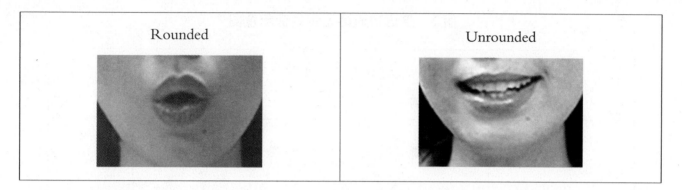

| Rounded | Unrounded |

The vertical position of the tongue refers to the tongue being close to the roof of the mouth or close to the floor of the mouth as shown below:

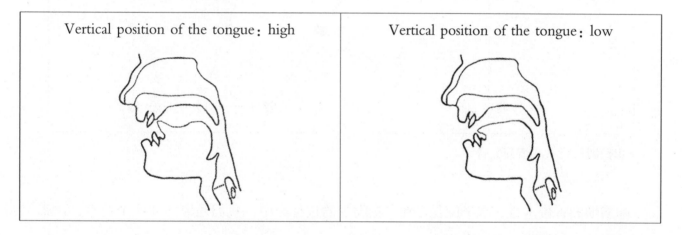

| Vertical position of the tongue: high | Vertical position of the tongue: low |

The horizontal position of the tongue refers to the tongue being close to the front teeth or close to the throat as shown below:

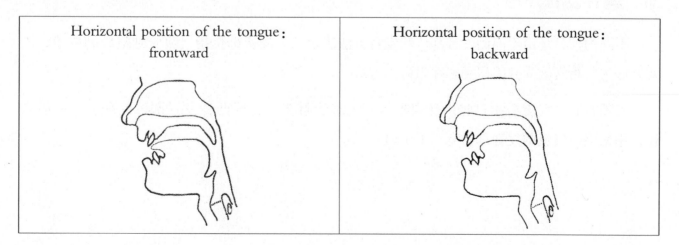

| Horizontal position of the tongue: frontward | Horizontal position of the tongue: backward |

根据唇形（圆唇、不圆唇），舌位的垂直位置（高、半高、半低、低），舌位的水平位置（前、中、后），汉语普通话中的 7 个基本元音可用图示意如下：

图 2　汉语普通话元音发音示意图

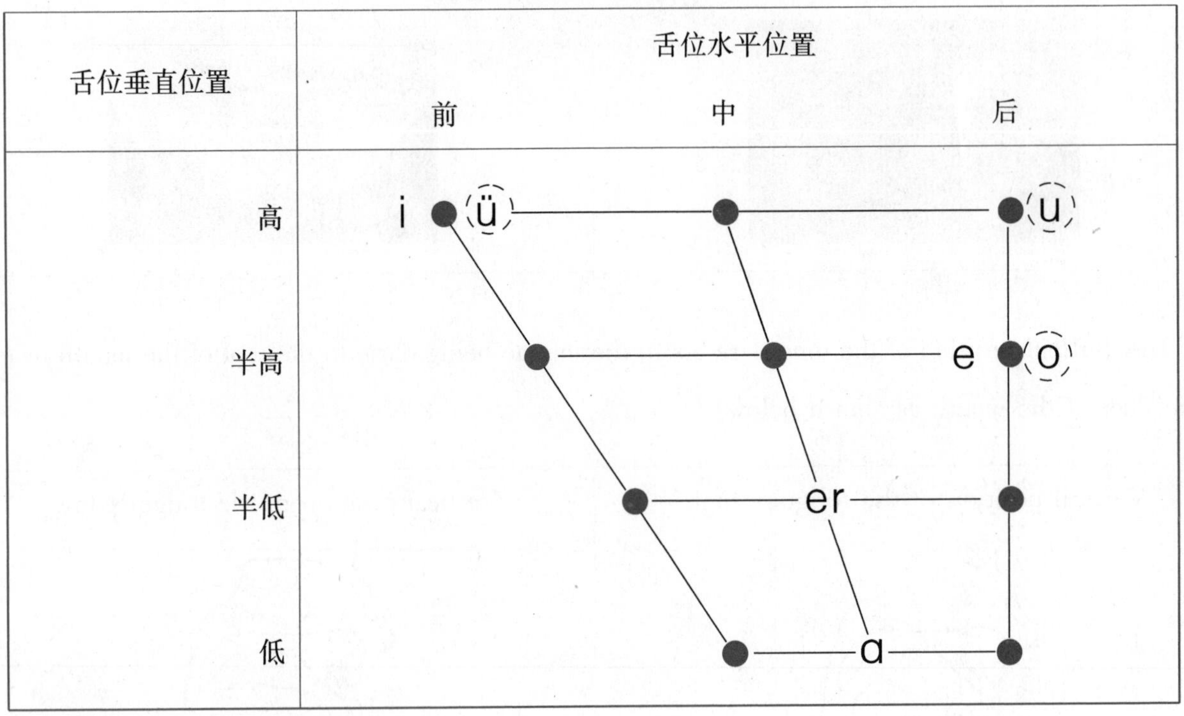

* 虚线圆形 ◯ 代表圆唇元音

除唇形和舌位垂直、水平位置之外，在发音的过程当中，我们还应注意两个要点：声带保持振动以及维持发音力度平衡。

Ⅲ. 辅音发音规则

不同的辅音是由不同的发音部位和发音方法决定的。发音部位指气流受到阻碍的位置，发音方法主要指气流受到阻碍和解除阻碍的方式。

发辅音时，气流会在口腔内受到阻碍，气流受阻至少需要两种发音部位的配合。一般来说，用来阻碍气流的发音部位有以下 7 对：

Based on the shape of the mouth (rounded, unrounded), the vertical position of the tongue (high, half-high, half-low, and low), and the horizontal position of the tongue (front, central, and back), the pronunciation of seven basic vowels in standard Chinese can be illustrated below:

Figure 2. Guide to the Standard Chinese Vowels Pronunciation

Vertical positions of the tongue	Horizontal position of the tongue		
	Front	Central	Back
High			
Half-High			
Half-Low			
Low			

* The dotted circle ◌ indicates the rounded vowel.

In addition to the shape of the mouth and the positions (both vertical and horizontal) of the tongue when producing a vowel, we also should bear two points in mind that the vocal cords are always vibrated and the articulatory strength is kept at a fixed level during the entire process of articulation.

III. How to pronounce consonants

The sounds for consonants are determined by the position where the exhaled air is blocked in the oral or nasal cavity, and the way the air is blocked or released.

In pronouncing Chinese consonants, the air stream usually is blocked in the oral cavity. The blocking of the air stream requires at least the cooperation of two articulators. Generally speaking, the blocking of the air stream in pronouncing different Chinese consonants is made by the seven pairs of articulators listed below:

双唇：b p m

上齿与下唇：f

舌尖与上齿龈：d t n l

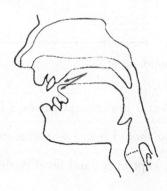

舌根与软腭：g k h ng

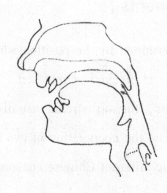

The two lips: b　p　m

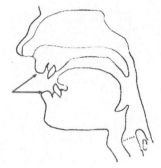

The upper teeth and the lower lip: f

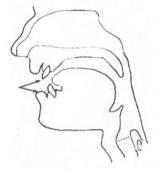

The tip of the tongue and the upper gum: d　t　n　l

The root of the tongue and the soft palate: g　k　h　ng

舌面与硬腭前部：j q x

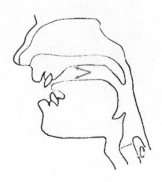

舌尖与硬腭前部：zh ch sh r

舌尖与上齿背或下齿背：z c s

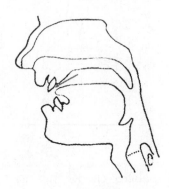

　　除了气流受阻的位置之外，不同的发音方法也会造成不同辅音，其要素主要包括气流受阻的程度（完全受阻或部分受阻）、气流受阻的变化、气流的强弱以及声带是否振动等。以后的课中将会引用下列术语来说明辅音的发音方法：

The surface of the tongue and the front part of the hard palate: j q x

The tip of the tongue and the front part of the hard palate: zh ch sh r

The tip of the tongue and the back of the upper teeth or lower teeth: z c s

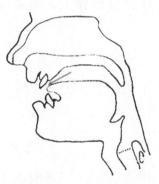

Besides the position of the air stream obstruction (the place where the air stream is blocked), other factors are also involved in the pronunciation of individual consonant, such as the degree of obstruction (the air stream is totally or partially blocked), the variation of the obstruction (the change in the degree of air stream obstruction during the process of pronunciation), the strength of the air stream (being weak or strong), and the degree of vibration of the vocal cords (being vibrated or not) etc. The following terms will be used in this textbook to describe the consonants' manner of articulation:

塞音：

口腔中构成阻碍的两个部分完全闭塞，瞬间压迫气流冲开阻碍形成塞音。

擦音：

口腔中构成阻碍的两个部分靠近，留下窄缝，气流从窄缝中挤出，与发音部位摩擦形成擦音。

塞擦音：

口腔中构成阻碍的两个部分先完全闭塞，再压迫气流把闭塞部分冲开一条窄缝，气流从窄缝中挤出，摩擦成声。

鼻音：

发鼻音时，口腔中形成阻碍的两个部分完全闭塞，气流从鼻腔中通过成声。

边音：

发边音时，气流并非从口腔中央部分释出，而是从舌头两边的空隙通过。

浊音/ 清音：

发浊音时声带随着气流的挤出而颤动，发清音时声带不颤动。

送气 / 不送气音：

发送气音时需呼出较强的气流，发不送气音时则不然。

表4 依据发音部位和发音方法列出了汉语普通话辅音的发音规则。

Plosive sound:

It is produced by completely blocking the air stream followed by a sudden release of the compressed air in the oral cavity.

Fricative sound:

It is produced when the two articulators involved form a narrow channel for the compressed air. During the pronunciation, the air stream meets increased resistance from the articulators and must be released with a strong force.

Affricate sound:

It is produced by first blocking the air stream and then by letting the air squeeze out through the narrow channel formed by the two articulators.

Nasal sound:

It is produced by totally blocking the air stream into the oral cavity and letting it out through the nasal cavity.

Lateral sound:

A lateral sound requires the air stream coming through the narrow channels on both sides of the tongue rather than through the center of the oral cavity.

Voiced vs. unvoiced sound:

A voiced sound requires the vibration of the vocal cord, while an unvoiced sound does not.

Aspirated vs. unaspirated sounds:

An aspirated sound requires a strong air stream while an unaspirated sound does not.

Based on the place of articulation and the manner of articulation, the rules of pronouncing each individual consonant are summarized in Table 4.

表4　汉语普通话辅音发音表

发音部位＼发音方法	塞音		擦音		塞擦音		鼻音	边音
	清音		清音	浊音	清音		浊音	浊音
	不送气	送气			不送气	送气		
双唇	b	p					m	
上齿与下唇			f					
舌尖与上齿龈	d	t					n	l
舌根与软腭	g	k	h				ng	
舌面与硬腭前部			x		j	q		
舌尖与硬腭前部			sh	r	zh	ch		
舌尖与上齿背			s		z	c		

Table 4.   Guide to the Standard Chinese Consonants Pronunciation

Manner / Position	Plosive Unvoiced Unasp.	Plosive Unvoiced Asp.	Fricative Unvoiced	Fricative Voiced	Affricate Unvoiced Unasp.	Affricate Unvoiced Asp.	Nasal Voiced	Lateral Voiced
Two lips	b	p					m	
Upper teeth & lower lip			f					
Tongue tip & upper gum	d	t					n	l
Tongue root & soft palate	g	k	h				ng	
Tongue surface & the front part of hard palate			x		j	q		
Tongue tip & the front part of hard palate			sh	r	zh	ch		
Tongue tip & back of upper teeth			s		z	c		

Note: Manner = The manner of articulation; Position = The position of articulation;

Unasp. = Unaspirated sound; and Asp. = Aspirated sound.

ā é ǚ
o í u

2

单韵母 a o e e r i u ü

声母 b p m f

a ó e i u ü

Simple Vowels a o e e r i u ü
Initial Consonants b p m f

第二课 单韵母 a o e e r i u ü
声母 b p m f

这一课介绍7个单韵母以及4个声母。解释发音时，在可能的情况下，我们将举出英文中相对应或相似的发音作为例子进行说明。

a

发音时，嘴张大，声带振动，舌头居中，舌位处于垂直位置的最低处，让气流自然释出。这个音与英文 **jar** 的最后一个音（加下划线的部分）的发音相似，但是汉语的"a"，舌位应比 jar 的"ar"再稍微往前一些。（见右页图1）

o

发音时，嘴唇圆拢，舌头向后缩并且隆起到半高的位置。这个音和英文 **log** 中的第二个音相近，然而汉语的"o"舌位比 log 的"o"高，而且唇形也较圆，不像 log 的"o"嘴唇是椭圆形的。（见右页图2）

e

发音时，唇形和舌位先与发"o"时相同，接着展唇成扁椭圆形。这个音很像英文 **bird** 的第二个音，不同处在于，汉语的"e"，舌位较高，唇形也更为扁平。（见右页图3）

er

"er"虽有两个字母，但它代表的只有一个音。发音时，唇形和舌位与发"e"时相同，但舌中部要稍微上抬，同时将舌尖向后卷。特别要注意的是舌位应保持在口腔正中央，不得接触其他部位。（见右页图4）

Lesson 2 Simple Vowels a o e e r i u ü
Initial Consonants b p m f

In this lesson, we will first learn seven simple vowels and four initial consonants . In explaining the pronunciation, we will provide English equivalents when possible.

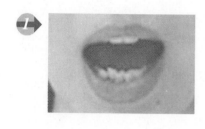

a   Open your mouth widely with tongue in the middle and its position in the lowest vertically. Let the air stream out naturally. This sound is close to the last sound (underlined) of **jar**, but the tongue position for Chinese "a" is slightly more forward than that of "ar" in *jar*.

a

o   Contract the tongue toward the root direction and at the same time raise the tongue to the half-high position and round your lips. This sound is close to the second sound in **log**. However, the tongue position for Chinese "o" is higher than that of "o" in *log*, and the mouth shape for Chinese "o" is not an oblong circle as in *log* but a perfect circle.

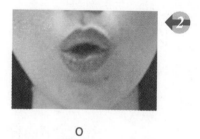

o

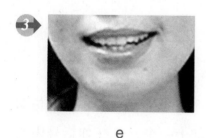

e

e   Make the shape of your lips and tongue position as in pronouncing "o", then change your lip shape to a very flat o-val. This sound is close to the second sound in **bird**, except the tongue position for Chinese "e" is slightly higher and the mouth shape is flatter than that of "ir" in *bird*.

er   The two letters form a single sound. Put your tongue and lip in position as when pronouncing Chinese "e", then raise the middle part of your tongue slightly and at the same time roll up the tip of your tongue backward. Make sure the position of your tongue stays in the middle of the oral cavity and touches nowhere.

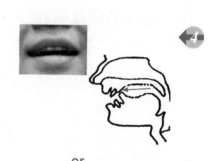

er

i

发音时，舌尖向前抬高并接触下齿背，同时展唇，嘴角往两边咧开。韵母"i"和英文 **east** 的第一个音是一样的。（见右页图5）

u

"u"的发音要领是舌头后缩，舌尖放低，两唇收缩成小椭圆形，略向前突出。这个韵母和英文 **moon** 的第二个音接近，差别在于，汉语"u"的舌位比较高，唇形也较圆。（见右页图6）

ü

先发"i"的音，然后将嘴唇逐渐收拢，由扁变圆，"ü"音便会被带出。英文里没有与"ü"相似的发音。（见右页图7）

下面介绍4个声母：b, p, m 和 f。声母皆为辅音，发辅音时，气流要受到各种不同部位的阻挡，声音轻短，不响亮，有点含糊。因此，我们在每个辅音之后加上一个元音（如括号内所示），使这些音听起来清晰和响亮一些。

i Place your tongue tip in the high position and it should touch the back of the lower front teeth, at the same time, stretch the corners of the mouth toward two sides. The simple vowel "i" is the same as the first sound in **east.**

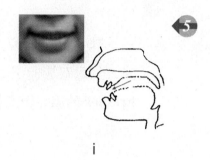

i

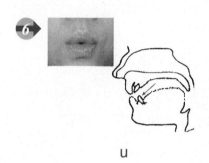

u

u Contract your tongue toward the root and keep the tongue tip in the low position. Make your mouth shape a small oval and protruding slightly. This simple vowel is close to the second sound in **moon**, but the tongue position for Chinese "u" is higher with more rounded mouth shape than that of "oo" in *moon*.

ü First, use the same tongue position as in pronouncing Chinese "i", then draw your lips in to form a perfect circle as small as possible. No English equivalent.

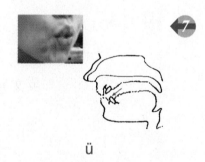

ü

Next, let us learn the four initial consonants: b, p, m and f. As we mentioned earlier, initials in Chinese *Pinyin* are all consonants and when pronouncing a consonant, the air stream initially is blocked in the oral cavity; therefore, the sound is light and short, not loud and clear. In order to make a resonant and clear consonant, we often add a vowel (as shown in the parentheses below) to a consonant, which will help us pronounce it clearly.

b (+O)

　　"b"是清塞音。在发"b"时，双唇闭合，气流受到双唇的阻挡而积蓄起来，然后双唇打开，让气流冲出，爆发而成不送气清塞音。这个音与英文 **b**rother 的第一个音相近，不同的是汉语的"b"是清音，声带不振动。(见右页图 8)

p (+O)

　　"p"也是清塞音。发"p"的阻碍部位和发音方法与发"b"同，只是在发"p"时，冲出的气流较强而成送气音。声母"p"和英文 **p**ie 的第一个音相似，注意汉语的"p"要送气。(见右页图 9)

m (+O)

　　"m"是鼻音。发音时，双唇闭合，气流从鼻腔出来，同时振动声带成声，声母"m"和英文 **m**ug 的第一个音相同。(见右页图 10)

f (+O)

　　"f"是清擦音。发音部位是上齿与下唇。在发"f"时，上齿与下唇相接，让气流从唇齿间的窄缝中挤出，摩擦成声。这是一个送气清音，与英文 **f**ar 的第一个音相同。(见右页图 11)

b (+ O)   It is an unvoiced plosive. Completely close both lips and then release the compressed air in the mouth suddenly to make an unaspirated unvoiced plosive. This sound is close to the first sound in **brother**, except that Chinese "b" is an unvoiced sound, thus the vocal cords do not vibrate.

b (波 bō wave)

p (+ O)   It is also an unvoiced plosive. Begin as in pronouncing "b". When pronouncing "p" sound, release the compressed air in the mouth to make an aspirated sound. This sound is similar to the first sound in **pie.** Pay attention that the "p" in Chinese is aspirated.

p (坡 pō slope)

m (+ O)   This is a nasal. When pronouncing this sound, close and press the lips initially and let the air out through the nose. Vibrate your vocal cords to make sound and it is the same as the first sound in **mug.**

m (墨 mò ink)

f (+ O)   This is an unvoiced fricative. The articulators involved in producing this sound are the upper front teeth and the lower lip. When pronouncing this sound, the upper front teeth touch the lower lip lightly and let the air escape through them. This is an unvoiced aspirated sound. This sound is the same as the first sound in **far.**

f (佛 fó Buddha)

Exercises 练习

A Write out the syllable according to the initial consonant and simple vowel given in the chart, and then read the syllable aloud.

根据下表提供的声母和韵母写出音节并朗读音节。

Initial consonants \ Simple vowels	a	o	e	er	i	u	ü
b	ba	--	--				--
p			--	--			--
m				--			--
f			--	--	--		--

Note：-- indicates no such syllable in standard Chinese.

B Read aloud the following syllables.

朗读下列音节。

1. ma   2. po   3. pa   4. bo
5. mu   6. mo   7. pi   8. bi
9. mi   10. fu   11. fa   12. pu

C Write out the initial consonant and simple vowel according to what you hear.

写出所听到的声母或韵母。

1. _____   2. _____   3. _____   4. _____   5. _____

6. _____   7. _____   8. _____   9. _____   10. _____

D Circle the initial consonant and simple vowel according to what you hear.

圈出所听到的声母或韵母。

Example：If you hear "a" please circle "a" in the list → e (a) i u o

1. er e o u a   2. i u a f ü   3. b p m o u
4. a u f b e   5. f o i ü u   6. e a i f b

E Draw a line to link the initial consonant and the simple vowel according to what you hear.

根据所听到的音节用线连接声母和韵母。

b   e
p   u
m   i
f   a
                     o

F Fill in the blanks according to the syllables you hear.

根据所听到的音节填空。

1. b____   2. p____   3. m____   4. f____
5. ____a   6. ____i   7. ____o   8. ____a

G Write out the sound according to what you hear.

写出所听到的拼音。

Group A. Initial consonants or simple vowels   声母或韵母

1. _____   2. _____   3. _____   4. _____   5. _____

6. _____   7. _____   8. _____   9. _____   10. _____

Group B. Syllables   音节

1. _____   2. _____   3. _____   4. _____   5. _____

6. _____   7. _____   8. _____   9. _____   10. _____

āáǎà éěè ōóǒò ǖǘǚǜ

3

声母 dtnlgkhjqx

第三课 声母 d t n l g k h j q x

这一课，我们将学习10个声母。

d (+e)

"d"是清塞音。发音部位是舌尖与上齿龈。在发"d"时，舌尖抵住上齿龈，先阻挡气流通过，然后让气流突然迸发而出，爆发成不送气清音。汉语的"d"与英文 dust 的第一个音相似，不同的是汉语的"d"是个清音。（见右页图1）

t (+e)

"t"也是清塞音。发音方法与发"d"类似，区别在于"d"是不送气清音，而"t"是送气清音。所以在发"t"时，冲出的气流比发"d"时要强许多。这个声母与英文 tide 的第一个音相似，注意汉语的"t"要送气。（见右页图2）

n (+e)

"n"是鼻音。发音部位是舌尖与上齿龈。在发"n"时，舌尖抵住上齿龈，完全阻挡口腔中的气流，让气流从鼻腔泄出，同时振动声带成声。这个音和英文 nation 的第一个音相同。（见右页图3）

Lesson 3   Initial Consonants d t n l g k h j q x

In this lesson, we'll learn the next ten initial consonants.

d (得 dé to get)

d (+ e)   This is an unvoiced plosive. The articulators involved in producing this sound are the tongue tip and the upper gum. First, block the air by pressing the tip of the tongue against the upper gum; then release the air suddenly to make an unvoiced unaspirated sound. This sound is similar to the first sound of **dust**, but "d" in Chinese is an unvoiced sound.

t (+ e)   This is also an unvoiced plosive. The way to produce this sound is similar to the Chinese "d". However, "d" is an unvoiced unaspirated sound while "t" is an unvoiced aspirated sound. Thus, when producing "t", you should make efforts to let air out with a strong pop. This sound is similar to the first sound of **tide.** Pay attention that the "t" in Chinese is aspirated.

t (特 tè special)

n (那 nà that)

n (+ e)   This is a nasal. The major articulators involved are the tip of tongue and the upper gum. When producing this sound, the tip of the tongue presses against the upper gum to completely block the air stream from the oral cavity and let the air out from the nose with vibrating vocal cords. This sound is the same as the first sound in **nation.**

l (+ e)

"l"是边音。"l"的发音方法与"n"类似,不同点是让气流从舌头两侧的空隙间流出而不是从鼻腔中出来。重点在于,发"l"时,舌尖抵住上齿龈,软腭上抬,使气流在口腔中并非完全受阻。英文 learn 的第一个音也是这样的发音方法。(见右页图4)

g (+ e)

"g"是清塞音。发音部位是舌根与软腭。在发"g"时,首先舌根隆起抵住软腭,封闭气流,然后舌位迅速下降,让气流迸出。这个声母与英文 grill 的第一个音相似,但是汉语的"g"是个清音。(见右页图5)

k (+ e)

"k"也是清塞音。"k"的发音方法与"g"类似,不同之处在于"k"是个送气音。这个声母跟英文 keg 的第一个音相似,只是在发汉语"k"时,冲出的气流要强得多。(见右页图6)

h (+ e)

"h"是清擦音。在发"h"时,软腭上升,舌根隆起,与软腭之间形成一个窄缝,气流从窄缝中泄出,摩擦成声。汉语"h"与英文 heart 的第一音相近,但要注意汉语"h"发音时的舌位要比英文的"h"更前一些。(见右页图7)

l (乐 lè happy)

l (+e)　This is a lateral. The manner of producing this sound is similar to the Chinese "n", except the air comes out from the two sides of the tongue instead of from the nose. When producing this sound, the tip of the tongue presses against the upper gum and the soft palate raises. Thus, the air stream is not totally blocked in the oral cavity. This sound is the same as the first sound in **learn.**

g (+e)　This is an unvoiced plosive. The articulators involved in producing this sound are the root of the tongue and the soft palate. When producing this sound, first, raise the root of the tongue and let it touch the soft palate; then stop the air stream, lower your tongue quickly and let the air out. This sound is similar to the first sound in **gill**, except the Chinese "g" is an unvoiced sound.

g (鸽 gē dove)

k (窠 kē nest)

k (+e)　This is also an unvoiced plosive. The manner of producing this sound is the same as the Chinese "g" except this is an aspirated sound. This sound is very similar to the first sound in **keg** except Chinese "k" is a more explosive sound.

h (+e)　This is an unvoiced fricative. When producing this sound, let the air out through the narrow channel which is formed by holding the root of your tongue slightly apart from the rising soft palate. This sound is similar to the first sound of **heart**, except the place of articulation for the Chinese "h" is more forward than that of the "h" in *heart*.

h (喝 hē drink)

j (+ i)

　　"j"是清塞擦音。发音部位是舌面前部与硬腭前部。在发"j"时，将舌面前部先抵住硬腭前部阻挡气流，接着再离开硬腭轻触下齿背，形成一个窄缝。与此同时，气流从窄缝中泄出，摩擦成声。这个声母和英文 **jeep** 的第一个音相似，但是汉语"j"发音时的舌位要比 jeep 当中的"j"高，且"j"的舌面是平的；除此以外，汉语的"j"是个清音，jeep 的"j"则是浊音。（见右页图 8）

q (+ i)

　　"q"也是清塞擦音。"q"的发音部位和发音方法与"j"相同，但是"q"是送气音。英文里没有与"q"相对应的发音。（见右页图 9）

x (+ i)

　　"x"是清擦音。"x"的发音部位和"j"、"q"相同。在发"j"和"q"时，气流先受阻再泄出；反之，发"x"时气流在口腔中从头到尾畅行无阻。英文里没有与"x"相对应的发音。（见右页图 10）

j (鸡 jī rooster)

j (+i)   This is an unvoiced affricate. The articulators involved in producing this sound are the front part of the tongue and the front part of the hard palate. First, raise the front part of the tongue to touch the hard palate; then, let the tip of your tongue touch the back of the lower teeth and produce this sound by letting the air squeeze out between the surface of the tongue and the hard palate. This sound is similar to the first sound of **jeep**. However, the tongue position for the Chinese "j" is higher and the tongue is flatter than that of the first sound in *jeep*. In addition, the Chinese "j" is an unvoiced sound while "j" in *jeep* is a voiced sound.

q (+i)   This is also an unvoiced affricate. The manner and place of articulation are the same as in pronouncing the Chinese "j". However, "q" is an aspirated sound. There is no equivalent in English.

q (七 qī seven)

x (西 xī west)

x (+i)   This is an unvoiced fricative. The place of articulation involved in producing this sound is the same as those in producing "j" and "q". However, for "j" and "q", the air stream initially is blocked and then forced out, while pronouncing "x", the air stream is not blocked during the whole pronunciation process. There is no equivalent in English.

Exercises 练习

A Write out the syllable according to the initial consonant and simple vowel given in the chart, and then read the syllable aloud.

根据下表提供的声母和韵母写出音节并朗读音节。

Initial consonants \ Simple vowels	a	o	e	er	i	u	ü
d	da	--		--			--
t		--		--			--
n		--		--			
l		--		--			
g		--		--	--		--
k		--		--	--		--
h		--		--	--		--
j	--	--	--	--		--	
q	--	--	--	--		--	
x	--	--	--	--		--	

B Read aloud the following syllables.

朗读下列音节。

1. da
2. te
3. le
4. ku
5. ji
6. ni
7. ge
8. qu
9. xu
10. ka
11. gu
12. he

C Write out the initial consonant according to what you hear.

写出所听到的声母。

1. _____ 2. _____ 3. _____ 4. _____ 5. _____

6. _____ 7. _____ 8. _____ 9. _____ 10. _____

D Circle the initial consonant according to what you hear.

圈出所听到的声母。

Example：If you hear "n" please circle "n" in the list → t ⓝ k j q

1. l g h t n   2. d h n k g   3. j q x t h
4. h t l g d   5. x q j t d   6. t n h x q

E Draw a line to link the initial consonant and the simple vowel according to what you hear.

根据所听到的音节用线连接声母和韵母。

d	e		n	a
g	a		k	i
h	u		j	ü（u）
t	i		q	o
l	o		x	e

F Fill in the blanks according to the syllables you hear.

根据所听到的音节填空。

1. l____   2. g____   3. t____   4. n____
5. ____i   6. ____u   7. ____e   8. ____u

G Write out the sound according to what you hear.

写出所听到的拼音。

Group A. Initial consonants or simple vowels　声母或韵母

1. _____   2. _____   3. _____   4. _____   5. _____

6. _____   7. _____   8. _____   9. _____   10. _____

Group B. Syllables　音节

1. _____   2. _____   3. _____   4. _____   5. _____

6. _____   7. _____   8. _____   9. _____   10. _____

Ràokǒulìng

绕口令 Tongue Twister

É hé Tù
鹅 和 兔
A Goose and a Rabbit

Hé li de é,
河 里 的 鹅,
A goose is in the river,

Bù kě bú è,
不 渴 不 饿,
Neither thirsty nor hungry,

Lèhēhē.
乐 呵 呵。
Aha… aha… aha.

Dì li de tù,
地 里 的 兔,
A rabbit is in the field,

Kè dà húlu,
嗑 大 葫 芦,
Nibbling a big calabash,

Bù tǔ pí.
不 吐 皮。
Spitting no skin.

4

声母　z c s zh ch sh r

Initial Consonants　z c s zh ch sh r

第四课 声母 z c s zh ch sh r

这一课我们学习 7 个声母。加在这些声母之后的元音"-i"和韵母"i"是不一样的。"-i"是附加在声母 z，c，s，zh，ch，sh 和 r 后头的特殊元音。当舌尖与上齿龈或硬腭形成一个通道，让气流从通道中通过并让声带振动，"-i"这个音就会被带出。

z (+ -i)

"z"是清塞擦音。发音部位是舌尖与上齿背。发音时，舌尖先抵住上齿背，再迅速将舌尖稍微后移，形成一个窄缝，让气流从窄缝中挤出。声母"z"与英文 **zero** 的第一个音相近，细微差别在于 zero 的"z"是浊塞擦音，而汉语声母"z"是清塞擦音。（见右页图 1）

c (+ -i)

"c"也是清塞擦音。"c"的发音方法与"z"非常接近，唯一的区别是"z"是不送气清音，而"c"是送气音。因此，发"c"挤出的气流比发"z"时要强许多。声母"c"和英文 **students** 的最后一个音相似。（见右页图 2）

s (+ -i)

"s"是清擦音。发音部位是舌尖与下齿背。发音时，舌尖触及下齿背，让气流从舌面与上齿间的窄缝挤出。声母"s"是个清音。它与英文**students** 的第一个音发音相同。（见右页图 3）

Lesson 4 Initial Consonants z c s zh ch sh r

In this lesson, we will learn another seven initial consonants. The vowel "-i" added to these initial consonants is not the same as "i". The sound "-i" is a special Chinese vowel that only goes with z, c, s, zh, ch, sh, and r. The sound is made when the tip of the tongue and the upper gum or the hard palate form an air channel and let the air out through the channel with vibrating vocal cords.

z (子 zǐ son)

z (+ -i)   This is an unvoiced affricate. The articulators involved in this sound are the tip of the tongue and the back of the upper teeth. It is produced by initially pressing the tip of the tongue against the back of the upper teeth; then quickly moving the tongue tip backward to leave a channel and let the air squeeze out. This sound is similar to the first sound in **zero**. The only difference is that "z" in *zero* is a voiced affricate, while Chinese "z" is an unvoiced one.

c (+ -i)   This is also an unvoiced affricate. The manner of articulation is very similar to the Chinese initial consonant "z". The only difference is that "z" is an unaspirated unvoiced sound while "c" is an aspirated unvoiced one. Thus, you produce the "c" sound with much more breath. This sound is very similar to the last sound of **students.**

c (瓷 cí porcelain)

s (寺 sì temple)

s (+ -i)   This is an unvoiced fricative. The articulators involved are the tip of the tongue and the back of the lower teeth. When producing this sound, let the tip of the tongue touch the back of the lower teeth, at the same time, let the air squeeze out between the surface of the tongue and the upper teeth. This is an unvoiced sound and is the same as the first sound of **students.**

zh (+ -i)

　　"zh"是清塞擦音。发音部位是舌尖后端与硬腭。在发"zh"时，舌尖翘起，接近并且微离硬腭，形成一个窄缝，压迫气流从窄缝中挤出成声。英文里没有与"zh"相似的发音。（见右页图4）

ch (+ -i)

　　"ch"也是清塞擦音。"ch"的发音方法与汉语声母"zh"非常接近，但是"ch"是送气音，所以发音时挤出的气流更为强劲。（见右页图5）

sh (+ -i)

　　"sh"是清擦音。发音部位是舌尖后端与硬腭。在发音时，舌尖翘起，靠近硬腭，在舌尖与硬腭之间留一个窄缝，让气流从缝间挤出成声。英文里没有与"sh"相对应的发音。（见右页图6）

zh (+ -i)　　This is an unvoiced affricate. The articulators involved in producing this sound are the back end of the tongue tip and the hard palate. It is produced by initially rolling up the tip of the tongue close to the hard palate, then forcing the air out through the narrow channel between the tongue and the hard palate. No equivalent sound in English.

zh （指 zhǐ finger）

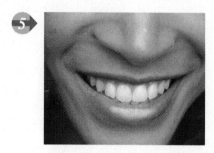

ch （齿 chǐ tooth）

ch (+ -i)　　This is also an unvoiced affricate. The method of producing this sound is very similar to the Chinese "zh" except it is an aspirated sound; thus, you must produce this sound with more breath. No English equivalent.

sh (+ -i)　　This is an unvoiced fricative. The articulators involved in producing this sound are the back end of the tongue tip and the hard palate. The sound is produced by rolling up the tip of the tongue very close to the hard palate without totally blocking the area and letting the air squeeze out through the channel. No equivalent sound in English.

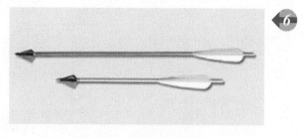

sh （矢 shǐ arrow）

zh, ch, sh 和 z, c, s 这两类声母最大的差别在于,前者是卷舌音,后者则不然。下图可以帮助我们更清楚地看出这两类声母发音时舌位的不同。

z c s 和 zh ch sh 发音对比

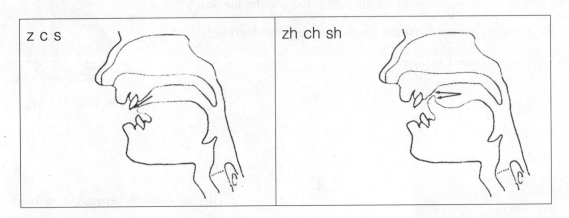

r (+ -i)

"r"是浊擦音。发音部位是舌尖与硬腭前端。发音时,舌尖朝硬腭前端翘起,然后轻触硬腭前端,最后压迫气流让它从舌尖与硬腭间的窄缝挤出,同时振动声带,摩擦成声。(见右页图7)

The major difference in the pronunciation of the two groups of zh, ch, sh and z, c, s is that zh, ch, sh are retroflex sound (which requires the rolling up of the tongue when producing them) while z, c, s are not. The figure below highlights the difference of the tongue positions in pronouncing these two groups of sounds.

Pronunciation Comparisons between z c s **and** zh ch sh

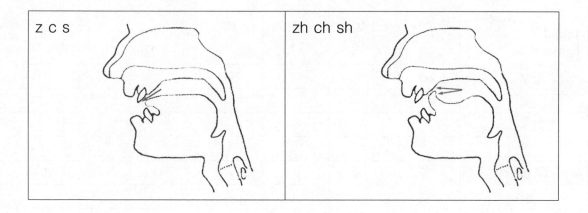

r (+ -i)   This is a voiced fricative. The articulators involved in producing this sound are the tip of the tongue and the front end of the hard palate. The sound is produced by rolling up the tip of tongue toward the front end of the hard palate. Then let the tongue tip touch the hard palate lightly. Finally, let the air squeeze out between the tongue tip and the hard palate while vibrating the vocal cords.

r (日 rì sun)

Exercises 练习

A Write out the syllable according to the initial consonant and simple vowel given in the chart, and then read the syllable aloud.

根据下表提供的声母和韵母写出音节并朗读音节。

Initial consonants \ Simple vowels	a	o	e	er	-i	u	ü
z	za	--		--			--
c		--		--			--
s		--		--			--
zh		--		--			--
ch		--		--			--
sh		--		--			--
r	--	--		--			--

B Read aloud the following pairs of syllables.

朗读下列音节。

1. ci—chi 2. se—she 3. za—zha 4. zhe—ze
5. chu—cu 6. sha—sa 7. ri—re 8. shu—su
9. si—shi 10. zha—cha 11. chi—shi 12. zhe—che

C Write out the initial consonant according to what you hear.

写出所听到的声母。

1. _____ 2. _____ 3. _____ 4. _____ 5. _____

6. _____ 7. _____ 8. _____ 9. _____ 10. _____

D Circle the initial consonant according to what you hear.

圈出所听到的声母。

Example：If you hear "z" please circle "z" in the list → s (z) c zh ch

1. r sh s z zh   2. zh r z c s   3. ch c r sh z

4. sh c s ch r   5. c ch s sh zh   6. sh ch r zh ch

E Draw a line to link the initial consonant and the simple vowel according to what you hear.

根据所听到的音节用线连接声母和韵母。

zh	e	ch	a
c	a	j	o
s	u	b	i
r	i	sh	ü(u)
z	o	x	e

F Fill in the blanks according to the syllables you hear.

根据所听到的音节填空。

1. r ____   2. ch ____   3. s ____   4. zh ____

5. ____ i   6. ____ a   7. ____ e   8. ____ u

G Write out the sound according to what you hear.

写出所听到的拼音。

Group A. Initial consonants or simple vowels   声母或韵母

1. _____   2. _____   3. _____   4. _____   5. _____

6. _____   7. _____   8. _____   9. _____   10. _____

Group B. Syllables   音节

1. _____   2. _____   3. _____   4. _____   5. _____

6. _____   7. _____   8. _____   9. _____   10. _____

11. _____   12. _____

 **Tongue Twister**

Sì hé Shí
四 和 十
Four and Ten

Sì shì sì,
四 是 四,
Four is four,

Shí shì shí.
十 是 十。
And ten is ten.

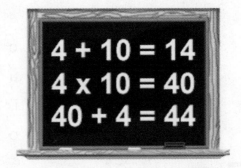

Sì jiā shí shì shí sì,
四 加 十 是 十四,
Four plus ten equals fourteen,

Sì chéng shí shì sì shí,
四 乘 十 是 四十,
And four times ten is forty,

Sì shí jiā sì shì sì shí sì.
四十 加 四 是 四十四。
Forty plus four is forty-four.

5

声 调

āáǐ ǔu

Tones

第五课 声 调

这一课我们学习汉语普通话的四声与轻声。

汉语是声调语言。根据调值，现代汉语普通话的基本声调可归为四类：阴平（高平调），阳平（高升调），上声（降升调），去声（全降调）。亦可依序称为一声、二声、三声和四声。这四个声调的调值图示如下：

汉语普通话四声调值图

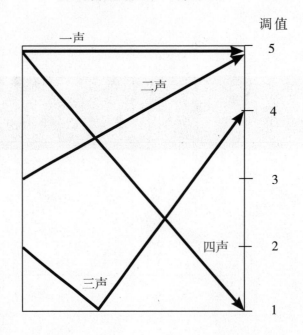

发音时，第一声的调值从头到尾始终维持在音高的最高等级5；第二声的起始音高为3，逐渐往上高升至5；第三声则是从2出发，往下降到1，再上升到4的位置；第四声从音高5开始，一路降到1。我们用声调符号－ˊˇˋ分别代表不同调值的四个声调。

Lesson 5 Tones

In this lesson we will study the four basic tones and the neutral(zero) tone in standard Chinese.

Different from English, Chinese is a tonal language. Based on tone pitch, the basic tones in standard Chinese can be classified into four types: high level tone, high rising tone, fall-rise tone and high falling tone. They can also be called as the first tone, second tone, third tone and fourth tone. The tone pitch for each of the four tones is illustrated in the figure below.

Tone Pitches of the Four Tones in the Standard Chinese

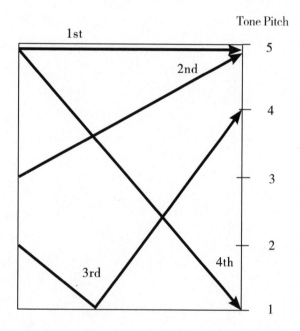

For the first tone, the tone pitch starts from 5 and keeps at this level until it finishes. The second tone initially starts at 3 and then gradually rises to 5. The third tone starts from 2 and drops down to 1, then rises up to 4. The fourth tone starts at 5 and drops down to 1. The tone marks for the four tones are written as ⁻, ╱, ⌄, ╲ respectively.

　　《汉语大字典》总共收录了 54，678 个汉字，这些汉字却只有 440 个不同的音节。也就是说，汉语里包含大量的同音字。声调能在一定程度上减少同音字对口头交流所带来的困扰。一个音节如果换了声调，音节所代表的意义也会随之改变，因此，声调在口语中具有区别意义的功能（见右页图）。同音字在书面语中并不造成麻烦，因为每一个同音字的字形都不同，所以即使是同音字，我们也能从汉字字形上区别其意义的不同。

　　除了四个声调之外，还有轻声。当一个音在语流中受到周围音节的影响而失去部分调值，只保留原调值的一小部分，就会导致调值的变化。变调后的音节比原调值的音节弱，也比原调值短，这样的声调我们称之为"轻声"或"零声调"。除了某些特定字词或是某些字词在特定的句子中轻读以外，汉语的助词大多读作轻声。我们将在第十课中进一步讨论汉语的轻声。

The *Comprehensive Chinese Characters Dictionary* (1992) has a total of 54, 678 Chinese character entries, but these characters are represented by only about 440 syllables. That means there are considerable homophones in Chinese. The introduction of the four tones into the Chinese syllables greatly eliminates the confusion caused by homophones. Consequently, a change in tone in a spoken syllable will bring about a change in the meaning denoted by that syllable, which is indicated in the examples below:

mā	má	mǎ	mà
妈	麻	马	骂
mother	linen	horse	to scold

However, in written Chinese, such confusion is impossible, for virtually all characters with the same pronunciation are represented with different written forms.

Besides the four basic tones, there is a neutral tone in Chinese. It occurs when a sound loses its inherent tone due to the influence of the surrounding syllables. In this case, it will no longer be pronounced with its original tone pitch; rather, only part of the inherent tone is retained, which makes the sound of the syllable much weaker and the tone pitch much shorter than that of the original. That is, the tone of the particular syllable has been altered. We call such altered pronunciation neutral tone. In addition to the syllables in particular words or sentences which have neutral tones, the tones of the Chinese particles are always pronounced in neutral tones. We will discuss this in detail in Lesson 10.

Exercises 练习

A Read aloud the following pairs of syllables and pay attention to their different tones.

朗读下列各组音节，注意声调的不同。

1. ā—á	2. ó—ò	3. ē—ě	4. ér—èr	5. ī—ǐ
6. ū—ǔ	7. ǔ—ù	8. gé—gè	9. hǔ—hù	10. qū—qù
11. mǒ—mò	12. lā—là	13. zhě—zhè	14. sū—sù	15. chí—chǐ
16. rě—rè	17. mó—mò	18. dē—dé	19. mā—mǎ	20. lē—lè

B Read aloud the following syllables.

朗读下列音节。

1. mùlù	2. fǎlǜ	3. qíjì	4. fùmǔ	5. érnǚ
6. rìlì	7. gēqǔ	8. nítǔ	9. shùmù	10. lìqì

C Circle the syllable according to what you hear.

圈出所听到的音节。

Example：If you hear "má" please circle "má" in the list. → mā (má) mǎ mà

1. gē gé gě gè   2. qū qú qǔ qù   3. cī cí cǐ cì

4. mō mó mǒ mò   5. shā shá shǎ shà   6. zū zú zǔ zù

D Add tone marks to the following syllables according to what you hear.

根据所听到的录音为下列音节标上声调。

1. quzhe	2. dadi	3. pifu	4. duli	5. nali
6. zhuzhi	7. shige	8. richu	9. timu	10. ziju

E Write out the syllable with its tone mark according to what you hear.

写出所听到的音节并标上声调。

Group A. Monosyllables   单音节

1. _____   2. _____   3. _____   4. _____

5. _____   6. _____   7. _____   8. _____

Group B. Polysyllables   多音节

1. _____   2. _____   3. _____   4. _____

5. _____   6. _____   7. _____   8. _____

9. _____   10. _____   11. _____   12. _____

Ràokǒulìng

绕口令 Tongue Twister

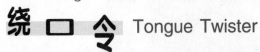

Yéye Bǎi Tānzi
爷爷 摆 摊子
Grandpa Sets up a Stall

Yéye bǎi tānzi,
爷爷 摆 摊子,
Grandpa sets up a stall,

Mài qiézi、 júzi hé xiézi.
卖 茄子、 橘子 和 鞋子。
and sells eggplants, oranges and shoes.

Màiwánle qiézi mài júzi,
卖完了 茄子 卖 橘子,
After selling out the eggplants he sells oranges,

Màiwánle júzi mài xiézi,
卖完了 橘子 卖 鞋子,
After selling out the oranges he sells shoes,

Màiwánle xiézi, yéye hēng qǔzi.
卖完了 鞋子, 爷爷 哼 曲子。
After selling out the shoes grandpa sings.

6

复元音韵母　ai ei ao ou ia ie ua uo üe

Compound Vowels　ai ei ao ou ia ie ua uo üe

第六课 复元音韵母　ai ei ao ou ia ie ua uo üe

这一课，我们学习 9 个复韵母。

ai

这是一个前响复韵母。"前响"指的是该复韵母的第一个音发得比第二个响而且长。发"ai"音时注意，这个复韵母中的"a"音和单韵母"a"音类似，只是开口度比单韵母"a"稍微小一点，发出"a"音后，逐渐收敛口型并很轻很短地发出单韵母"i"音。复韵母"ai"音和英文字母 I 音非常接近，不过英文 I 的开口度更大，其尾音也更长，汉语"ai"第一个音"a"响且长，随后的"i"轻且短。(见右页图 1)

ei

这是一个前响复韵母。发音时注意，嘴巴张开至发单韵母"a"的一半处，发出"ei"音中的第一个音，然后逐渐收敛口型并很轻很短地发出单韵母"i"音。复韵母"ei"音和英文字母 A 音非常接近，细微的差别在于，英文字母 A 音中包含的两个音是几乎一样长、一样响的，而汉语"ei"音中的"e"音比"i"音响且长。(见右页图 2)

Lesson 6   Compound Vowels   ai ei ao ou ia ie ua uo üe

In this lesson, we will learn nine compound vowels. In the subsequent text, we just use "compound" for short.

ai（爱 ài love）

ai   This is a falling compound. "Falling" means that the first sound of the compound is pronounced louder with longer duration than the second sound. In producing "ai", the "a" sound in "ai" is similar to the simple vowel "a", except that the mouth is opened slightly smaller than the simple vowel "a". As soon as the "a" sound is made, close the mouth gradually to the position of producing another simple vowel "i", and pronounce the "i" very shortly and lightly. This sound is very similar to the sound of English letter **I**. However, English *I* has a wider opening of the mouth and longer ending sound. For Chinese "ai", the "a" is louder and longer while the "i" is very light and short.

ei   This is a falling compound. When producing the first part of "ei", the openness of the mouth is about half of that for producing the simple vowel "a", then gradually switch to the position of producing another simple vowel "i", and pronounce it shortly and lightly. This sound is very similar to the English letter **A**. The slight difference between them is that when producing *A*, the duration and loudness of the first and second sounds are almost equal, but for Chinese "ei", the first sound "e" is longer and louder than the second sound "i".

ei（杯 bēi cup）

ao

  这是一个前响复韵母。发音时先发出单韵母"a"音，然后改变口型发出"u"音。"a"音应该响且长，而"u"音应该轻且短。复韵母"ao"音和英文 **doubt** 中的双元音"ou"很接近，不过发汉语"ao"时开口度较英文 doubt 中的"ou"音小，此外，中文"ao"的第一个音"a"响且长，随后的"u"轻且短，而英文 doubt 中"ou"音"o"和"u"响度和长度相当。（见右页图 3）

ou

  这是一个前响复韵母。发第一个音时张开嘴，口型应该比单韵母"a"小，比单韵母"o"宽，然后改变口型发出"u"音。第一个音应该比第二个音响且长。双韵母"ou"和英文 **oh** 很接近，区别在于发汉语"ou"音时，舌头的位置比发英文 oh 略前；还有，汉语"ou"音的第一个音比第二个音响且长，而英文 oh 这种情况不明显。（见右页图 4）

ia

  这是一个后响复韵母。"后响"指的是该复韵母的第二个音发得比第一个响而且长。发"ia"音时注意，先发单韵母"i"，然后过渡到"a"音。记住，第一个音"i"应该轻且短，第二个音"a"则响且长。（见右页图 5）

ao（袄 ǎo Chinese-
style coat）

ao This is a falling compound. First, pronounce the simple vowel "a" and gradually switch to the sound "u". The "a" should be produced louder and longer while "u" is lighter and shorter. This compound "ao" is similar to the diphthong in **doubt**, but Chinese "ao" requires a smaller opening of the mouth than "ou" in *doubt*, and also Chinese "ao" requires producing the first sound of "ao" longer and louder than the second sound. While producing "ou" in *doubt*, the duration and loudness for "o" and "u" are equal.

ou This is a falling compound. It is produced by opening the mouth to a point which is smaller than the simple vowel "a" but wider than the simple vowel "o", then gradually switch to the position of producing the simple vowel "u". The first sound "o" should be produced louder and longer than the following sound "u". This compound is similar to **oh** in English. However, when producing Chinese "ou" the tongue position is slightly more forward than that of the English *oh*. In addition, in Chinese "ou", the first sound "o" is louder and longer than the second sound "u", but there is no such noticeable difference in producing the English *oh*.

ou（鸥 ōu gull）

ia（鸭 yā duck）

ia This is a rising compound. Here, "rising" means the second sound of the compound is always pronounced louder and the duration of the sound is also longer than that of the first sound of the compound. When producing "ia", first pronounce the simple vowel "i" and then gradually switch to pronouncing another simple vowel "a". Since this is a rising compound, we must produce "i" with shorter and lighter sound than that of "a".

ie

　　这是一个后响复韵母。首先发出单韵母"i"音，然后半张开嘴到"a"音的一半位置，就形成了"ie"音。复韵母"ie"音和英文 **yell** 中"ye"音很接近，差别仅在于汉语"ie"的第一个音"i"轻且短，第二个音"e"则响且长，而英文词 yell 中"ye"没有这个特点。（见右页图6）

ua

　　这是一个后响复韵母。先发出单韵母"u"音，然后发出单韵母"a"音。"a"音比"u"音响而且长。（见右页图7）

uo

　　这是一个后响复韵母。先发出单韵母"u"音，然后发出单韵母"o"音。"o"音比"u"音响而且长。（见右页图8）

üe

　　这是一个后响复韵母。先发出单韵母"ü"音，然后朝两边轻轻展开嘴唇，口型开至"a"的一半宽，舌尖放低，触及下排牙齿齿龈稍下处。（见右页图9）

ie（叶 yè leaf）

ie This is a rising compound. First, pronounce the simple vowel "i"; then, open the mouth half way to the position when pronounce "a". This sound is similar to the English "ye" in **yell**. The only difference is that in pronouncing the Chinese "ie", "i" is shorter and lighter while "e" is longer and louder. There is no such difference in producing "ye" as in *yell*.

ua This is a rising compound. The sound can be firstly produced by pronouncing the simple vowel "u" then followed by another simple vowel "a". The "a" sound is louder and longer than the "u" sound.

ua（蛙 wā frog）

uo（蜗 wō snail）

uo This is a rising compound. First, pronounce the simple vowel "u", then, smoothly shift to pronounce another simple vowel "o". Remember to pronounce "o" louder and longer than "u".

üe This is a rising compound. First, produce the Chinese simple vowel "ü", then stretch the lips toward the sides slightly and open your mouth half wide as for "a", lower the tip of the tongue and let it touch the area which is slightly below the gum of the lower teeth.

üe（月 yuè moon）

Exercises 练习

A Write out the syllable according to the initial consonant and compound vowel given in the chart, and then read the syllable aloud.

根据下表提供的声母和韵母写出音节并朗读音节。

Initial consonants \ Compound vowels	ai	ei	ao	ou	ia	ie	ua	uo	üe
b	bai			--	--		--	--	--
p				--		--	--	--	
m				--		--	--	--	
f	--		--		--	--		--	
d						--	--		
t					--		--	--	
n					--		--		
l							--		
g					--	--			--
k					--	--			--
h					--	--			--
j	--	--	--	--			--	--	
q	--	--	--	--			--	--	
x	--	--	--	--			--	--	
z					--	--	--		--
c		--			--	--	--		--
s		--			--	--	--		--
zh					--	--			--
ch		--			--	--			--
sh					--	--			--
r	--	--			--	--	--		--

B Read aloud the following pairs of compound vowels.

朗读下列各组韵母。

1. ài — iǎ   2. ēi — iě   3. ǒu — uǒ

4. uā — üè   5. áo — ǎi   6. iǎ — iē

C Read aloud the following syllables.

朗读下列音节。

Group A. Monosyllables   单音节

1. huà   2. lóu   3. mài   4. xié   5. tuò   6. nüè   7. dāo   8. xià

9. kāi   10. lèi   11. guǒ   12. tiě   13. féi   14. pāo   15. jiā   16. hòu

Group B. Polysyllables   多音节

1. kǎoshì   2. kāishǐ   3. xuéxí   4. shuōhuà   5. lǎoshī

6. guójiā   7. měilì   8. gàosù   9. xià kè   10. xièxie

D Circle the compound vowel according to what you hear.

圈出所听到的韵母。

Example：If you hear "ao" please circle "ao" in the list → ai (ao) ou ua uo

1. ia ie ua ao üe   2. ao ou ua uo ai

3. ia ai ou ua ie   4. ua ei ou ie uo

5. üe ei ao ua ia   6. ai ao ia ie ua

E Draw a line to link the initial consonant and the simple or compound vowel according to what you hear.

根据所听到的音节用线连接声母和韵母。

d	é	zh	ěi
ch	āi	m	iè
h	ù	c	uō
s	ià	t	āo
x	óu	g	uā

F Fill in the blanks according to the syllables you hear and add tone marks on them.

根据所听到的音节填空并标上声调。

1. zh _____   2. g _____   3. r _____   4. j_____   5. c _____

6. _____ ie   7. _____ ua   8. _____ ei   9. _____ ai   10. _____ ou

G Write out the syllable with its tone mark according to what you hear.

写出所听到的音节并标上声调。

Group A. Monosyllables   单音节

1. _____   2. _____   3. _____   4. _____

5. _____   6. _____   7. _____   8. _____

Group B. Polysyllables   多音节

1. _____   2. _____   3. _____   4. _____   5. _____

6. _____   7. _____   8. _____   9. _____   10. _____

Ràokǒulìng
绕口令 Tongue Twister

Lánlan hé Nánnan
兰兰 和 南南
Lanlan and Nannan

Lánlan shì nǚháir,
兰兰 是 女孩儿,
Lanlan is a girl,

Nánnan shì nánháir.
南南 是 男孩儿。
And Nannan is a boy.

Lánlan jiā zhòng lánhuā,
兰兰 家 种 兰花,
Lanlan's family plants orchid,

Nánnan jiā zhòng nánguā.
南南 家 种 南瓜。
And Nannan's family grows pumpkin.

Lánhuā kāi báihuā,
兰花 开 白花,
Orchid blooms with white flowers,

Nánguā kāi huánghuā.
南瓜 开 黄花。
And pumpkin blooms with yellow flowers.

Lánlan ài Nánnan jiā de nánguā huā,
兰兰 爱 南南 家 的 南瓜 花,
Lanlan loves the pumpkin blossom at Nannan's home,

Nánnan ài Lánlan jiā de bái lánhuā.
南南 爱 兰兰 家 的 白 兰花。
And Nannan loves the orchid blossom at Lanlan's home.

āéū̇ü

7

复元音韵母　iao iou(iu) uai uei(ui)

Compound Vowels　iao iou(iu) uai uei(ui)

第七课 复元音韵母 iao iou（iu） uai uei（ui）

这一课，我们学习4个复韵母。

iao

这个复韵母是由"i"音和"ao"音合成的。所以先发单韵母"i"，再发复韵母"ao"。（见右页图1）

iou

这个复韵母前面加声母的时候简写为"iu"。发音时先发单韵母"i"，再发复韵母"ou"。（见右页图2）

uai

这个复韵母是由"u"音和"ai"音合成的。所以先发单韵母"u"，再发复韵母"ai"。（见右页图3）

uei

这个复韵母前面加声母的时候简写为"ui"。发音时先发单韵母"u"，再发复韵母"ei"。（见右页图4）

Lesson 7 Compound Vowels iao iou(iu) uai uei(ui)

In this lesson, we will learn another four compound vowels.

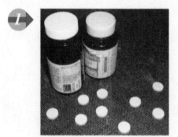

iao (药 yào medicine)

iao This complex vowel-compound is produced by pronouncing the Chinese simple vowel "i" first, followed by the compound "ao".

iou This complex vowel-compound is written as "iu" after an initial consonant. It is produced by pronouncing the Chinese simple vowel "i" first, followed by the compound "ou".

iou (油 yóu oil)

uai (外 wài outside)

uai This complex vowel-compound is produced by pronouncing the Chinese simple vowel "u" first, followed by the compound "ai".

uei This complex vowel-compound is written as "ui" after an initial consonant. Producing this sound requires pronouncing the Chinese simple vowel "u" first, followed by the compound "ei".

uei (喂 wèi Hello)

Exercises 练习

A Write out the syllable according to the initial consonant and compound vowel given in the chart, and then read the syllable aloud.

根据下表提供的声母和韵母写出音节并朗读音节。

Initial consonants \ Compound vowels	iao	iou (iu)	uai	uei (ui)
b	biao	--	--	--
p		--	--	--
m			--	--
f	--		--	--
d			--	
t		--		
n			--	--
l			--	
g	--	--		
k	--	--		
h	--	--		
j			--	--
q			--	--
x			--	--
z	--	--	--	
c	--	--	--	
s	--	--	--	
zh	--			
ch	--			
sh	--			
r	--	--	--	

B Read aloud the following compound vowels.

朗读下列韵母。

1. iao   2. ia   3. iou (iu)   4. ou   5. uai

6. uei (ui)   7. ua   8. uo   9. ao

C Read aloud the following syllables.

朗读下列音节。

Group A. Monosyllables   单音节

1. jiāo — liáo — xiǎo — piào   2. xiū — qiú — niǔ — jiù

3. guāi — huái — shuǎi — zhuài   4. huī — chuí — zuǐ — guì

Group B. Polysyllables   多音节

1. xuéxiào   2. kuàilè   3. jiàoshì   4. dǎ qiú   5. pái duì

6. qíguài   7. guǐguài   8. xiǎoniǎo   9. jiǔ bēi   10. xiū jià

D Draw a line to link the initial consonant and the compound vowel according to what you hear.

根据所听到的音节用线连接声母和韵母。

d	uí	zh	èi
ch	āi	h	iě
l	iù	c	uō
s	iào	t	ào
x	óu	n	uāi

E Fill in the blanks according to the syllables you hear and add tone marks on them.

根据所听到的音节填空并标上声调。

1. x _____   2. j _____   3. z _____   4. h _____   5. ch _____

6. _____ ao   7. _____ ai   8. _____ ui   9. _____ iu   10. _____ ao

F Write out the syllable with its tone mark according to what you hear.

写出所听到的音节并标上声调。

Group A. Monosyllables 单音节

1. _____   2. _____   3. _____   4. _____

5. _____   6. _____   7. _____   8. _____

Group B. Polysyllables 多音节

1. _____   2. _____   3. _____   4. _____   5. _____

6. _____   7. _____   8. _____   9. _____   10. _____

Shīgē
诗歌 Poem

Chūn Yè Xǐ Yǔ
春 夜 喜 雨
Welcome Rain on a Spring Night

Táng · Dù Fǔ
唐 · 杜 甫

Tang Dynasty · Du Fu

Hǎo yǔ zhī shíjié,
好 雨 知 时节,

The good rain knows its season.

Dāng chūn nǎi fā shēng.
当 春 乃 发 生。

When spring arrives, then it comes.

Suí fēng qiánrù yè,
随 风 潜入 夜,

It follows the wind secretly into the night,

Rùn wù xì wú shēng.
润 物 细 无 声。

And moistens all things softly without sound.

āéíöü

8

前鼻韵母　**an en in ün ian uan üan uen(un)**

Front Nasal Simple or Compound Vowels
an en in ün ian uan üan uen(un)

第八课 前鼻韵母 an en in ün ian uan üan uen（un）

这一课，我们介绍前鼻韵母。先让我们复习一下鼻音"n"的发音方法。

n

　　"n"是前鼻音。发这个音时主要靠舌尖和上排门牙后部这两个部位。舌尖抵住上排门牙的后部，在口腔里全面堵住来自喉管里的气流，让它从鼻腔里出来，并让声带振动。这个音和英文 **nation** 的第一个音相同。（见右页图1）

an

　　发这个音时，先把舌头置于发单韵母"a"的位置，然后舌尖微微向前，发出"a"音后紧接着发出鼻音"n"。这个音类似英文 **hand** 中的第二个音，不过汉语的"an"开口度比 hand 中的"an"大。（见右页图2）

en

　　发这个音时，先把舌头置于发单韵母"e"的位置，然后舌尖微微向前，发出"e"音后紧接着发出鼻音"n"。这个音类似英文 **Kentucky** 中的第二个音，只是汉语的"en"舌位稍偏后一点儿。（见右页图3）

Lesson 8 Front Nasal Simple or Compound Vowels

an en in ün ian uan üan uen(un)

In this lesson, we will introduce front nasal simple or compound vowels. Before learning these vowels, let us first review how the nasal sound "n" is made.

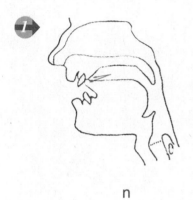

n

n This is a front nasal. The major articulators involved are the tip of the tongue and the back of the upper teeth. When producing this sound, the tip of the tongue presses against the back of the upper teeth to block the air stream completely from the trachea and let the air out from the nose with vibrating vocal cords. This sound is the same as the first sound in **nation**.

an Place the tongue in the position of producing the Chinese simple vowel "a" and then move the tip of your tongue slightly forward and produce the "a" sound followed by the nasal "n". This sound is similar to the second sound in **h<u>and</u>**; however, the Chinese "an" needs a wider opening of the mouth than the "an" sound in *hand*.

an (岸 àn shore)

en (摁 èn to press
with fingers/hands)

en Place the tongue in the position of producing the Chinese simple vowel "e", then move the tip of the tongue slightly forward to produce the first sound "e" followed by the nasal "n". This sound is similar to the "en" in **K<u>en</u>tucky**, except the tongue is slightly backward for the Chinese "en".

in

发这个音时，先发出单韵母"i"，紧接着发出鼻音"n"。这个音类似英文 **engage** 中的"en"音，不过汉语中的"in"开口度比 engage 中的"en"小。（见右页图4）

ün

发这个音时，先发出单韵母音"ü"，紧接着发出鼻音"n"。英文里没有与"ün"相似的发音。（见右页图5）

ian

发这个音时，先发出单韵母音"i"，紧接着发出"an"。（见右页图6）

uan

发这个音时，先发出单韵母音"u"，紧接着发出"an"。（见右页图7）

üan

发这个音时，先发出单韵母音"ü"，紧接着发出"an"。（见右页图8）

uen

这个前鼻韵母前面加声母的时候简写为"un"。发这个音时，先发出单韵母音"u"，紧接着发出"en"。（见右页图9）

4

in （印 yìn stamp）

in First produce the Chinese simple vowel "i", followed by pronouncing nasal "n". This sound is similar to the "en" in **engage**, except Chinese "in" has smaller opening of the mouth than the "en" in *engage*.

ün This sound is made by producing the Chinese simple vowel "ü" followed by the nasal "n". No equivalent in English.

 **5**

ün （云 yún cloud）

6

ian （烟 yān smoke/cigaret）

ian First produce the Chinese simple vowel "i", followed by "an".

uan First produce the Chinese simple vowel "u" firstly, followed by "an".

 **7**

uan （碗 wǎn bowl）

8

üan （圆 yuán circle）

üan First produce the Chinese simple vowel "ü", followed by "an".

uen This front nasal compound is written as "un" after an initial consonant. It is produced by pronouncing the Chinese simple vowel "u", followed by "en".

 **9**

uen （蚊 wén mosquito）

Exercises 练习

A Write out the syllable according to the initial consonant and front nasal simple or compound vowel given in the chart, and then read the syllable aloud.

根据下表提供的声母和韵母写出音节并朗读音节。

Initial consonants \ Front nasal simple or compound vowels	an	en	in	ün	ian	uan	üan	uen (un)
b	ban			--		--	--	--
p				--		--	--	--
m				--		--	--	--
f			--	--	--	--	--	--
d			--	--			--	
t		--	--	--			--	
n				--			--	--
l		--					--	
g			--	--	--		--	
k			--	--	--		--	
h			--	--	--		--	
j	--	--				--		--
q	--	--				--		--
x	--	--				--		--
z			--	--	--		--	
c			--	--	--		--	
s			--	--	--		--	
zh			--	--	--		--	
ch			--	--	--		--	
sh			--	--	--		--	
r			--	--	--		--	

B Read aloud the following pairs of front nasal simple or compound vowels.

朗读下列各组韵母。

1. an — en   2. in — ün   3. ian — uan

4. uan — un   5. ün — un   6. en — un

C Read aloud the following syllables.

朗读下列音节。

Group A. Monosyllables　单音节

1. mán — mián — mín — mén   2. juān — jūn — jiān — jīn

3. chén — chún — chán — chuán

Group B. Polysyllables　多音节

1. kùndùn   2. zhuānxīn   3. biànlùn   4. cúnqián   5. juānkuǎn

6. jīntiān   7. liánxì   8. bēnchí   9. rénqún   10. xīnnián

D Circle the front nasal simple or compound vowel according to what you hear.

圈出所听到的韵母。

Example：If you hear "an" please circle "an" in the list → en　un　in　ün　(an)

1. ian en uan in ün   2. an un in ian uan

3. ian uan un ün en   4. un en uan üan an

5. ün un in en an   6. an in ian üan un

E Draw a line to link the initial consonant and the compound vowel or the front nasal simple or compound vowel according to what you hear.

根据所听到的音节用线连接声母和韵母。

d	én	zh	uì
ch	āi	m	iě
h	ùn	c	án
s	iàn	t	uàn
x	óu	g	ǐn

F Fill in the blanks according to the syllables you hear and add tone marks on them.

根据所听到的音节填空并标上声调。

1. zh ____   2. g ____   3. r ____   4. j ____   5. s ____

6. ____ an   7. ____ uan   8. ____ en   9. ____ un   10. ____ ian

G Write out the syllable with its tone mark according to what you hear.

写出所听到的音节并标上声调。

Group A. Monosyllables　单音节

1. _____   2. _____   3. _____   4. _____

Grop B. Polysyllables　多音节

1. _____   2. _____   3. _____   4. _____

Shīgē
诗歌 Poem

Xuě Jǐng
雪 景
A Snow Scene

Qīng   Wúmíngshì
清 · 无名氏

Qing Dynasty · Anonymous

Yí piàn yí piàn yòu yí piàn,
一 片 一 片 又 一 片，

One flake, another flake, and another,

Sān piàn sì piàn wǔ liù piàn,
三 片 四 片 五 六 片，

Three, four, five, and six flakes,

Liù piàn qī piàn bā jiǔ piàn,
六 片 七 片 八 九 片，

Six, seven, eight, and nine flakes,

Fēirù lúhuā dōu bú jiàn.
飞入 芦花 都 不 见。

When flying into the reed marshes, they disappear.

āéū
aóü
oíu

9

后鼻韵母 ang eng ing ong iang uang iong ueng

Back Nasal Simple or Compound Vowels

ang eng ing ong iang uang iong ueng

第九课 后鼻韵母 ang eng ing ong iang uang iong ueng

这一课，我们要介绍后鼻韵母。首先，我们来学习怎样发后鼻音"ng"。

ng

"ng"是后鼻音。发这个音时，抬起舌根紧紧地顶压住软颚，在口腔里全面堵住喉管里的气流，让气流从鼻腔里出来，并让声带振动。（见右页图1）

ang

发这个音时，先简短地发出单韵母音"a"，紧接着发出后鼻音"ng"。（见右页图2）

eng

发这个音时，先把舌头置于发单韵母"e"的位置，然后舌尖微微向前，简短地发出"e"音后紧接着发出后鼻音"ng"。（见右页图3）

ing

发这个音时，先发出单韵母音"i"，紧接着发出后鼻音"ng"。（见右页图4）

Lesson 9 Back Nasal Simple or Compound Vowels
ang eng ing ong iang uang iong ueng

In this lesson, we will introduce back nasal simple or compound vowels. Before we learn this group of vowels, we need to learn how to pronounce the back nasal "ng".

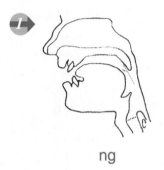

ng

ng "ng" is a back nasal. To produce this sound, raise the root of the tongue and press it against the soft palate tightly to block the air stream completely from the trachea. Then let the air out from the nasal cavity with vibrating vocal cords.

ang This sound is produced by pronouncing the Chinese simple vowel "a" shortly, followed by the back nasal "ng".

ang (昂 áng to hold one's head high)

eng (灯 dēng lamp)

eng First place the tongue in the position of pronouncing the Chinese simple vowel "e". Then move the tip of the tongue slightly forward by pronouncing the "e" in "eng" shortly, followed by the back nasal "ng".

ing This sound results from pronouncing the Chinese simple vowel "i", followed by the back nasal "ng".

ing (鹰 yīng hawk)

ong

发这个音时，先把舌头置于发单韵母"o"的位置，然后使开口度稍微增大一点，发出"ong"这个音的第一个音"o"，紧接着发出后鼻音"ng"。（见右页图5）

iang

发这个音时，先发出单韵母音"i"，紧接着发出"ang"。（见右页图6）

uang

发这个音时，先发出单韵母音"u"，紧接着发出"ang"。（见右页图7）

iong

发这个音时，先发出单韵母音"i"，紧接着发出"ong"。（见右页图8）

ueng

发这个音时，先发出单韵母音"u"，紧接着发出"eng"。（见右页图9）

5

ong (钟 zhōng clock)

ong Place the tongue in the position to pronounce the simple vowel "o", then open your mouth slightly wider to make the "o" sound in "ong" and quickly move to pronounce the back nasal "ng".

iang This sound comes by pronouncing the simple vowel "i", followed by the "ang" sound.

 6

iang (羊 yáng sheep)

7

uang (网 wǎng net)

uang This sound comes by pronouncing the simple vowel "u", followed by the "ang" sound.

iong This sound comes by pronouncing the single vowel "i", followed by the "ong" sound.

 8

iong (泳 yǒng to swim)

9

ueng (翁 wēng old man)

ueng This sound is produced by pronouncing the simple vowel "u", followed by the "eng" sound.

Exercises 练习

A Write out the syllable according to the initial consonant and back nasal simple or compound vowel given in the chart, and then read the syllable aloud.

根据下表提供的声母和韵母写出音节并朗读音节。

Back nasal simple or compound vowels / Initial consonants	ang	eng	ing	ong	iang	uang	iong	ueng
b	bang			--	--	--	--	--
p				--	--	--	--	--
m				--	--	--	--	--
f			--	--				
d				--				
t				--				
n					--	--		
l					--	--		
g			--		--			
k			--		--			
h			--		--			
j	--	--		--		--		
q	--	--		--		--		
x	--	--		--		--		
z			--		--		--	
c			--		--		--	
s			--		--		--	
zh			--		--		--	
ch			--		--		--	
sh			--	--	--		--	
r			--		--		--	--

B Read aloud the following pairs of back nasal simple or compound vowels.

朗读下列各组韵母。

1. āng — èng   2. ǐng — ōng   3. iáng — uǎng

4. iòng — uēng   5. áng — iáng   6. ōng — iǒng

C Read aloud the following syllables.

朗读下列音节。

Group A. Monosyllables   单音节

1. dāng — dēng — dīng — dōng   2. jiǎng — huáng — qióng — mèng

3. chuáng — làng — róng — xīng   4. shēng — cáng — liàng — guǎng

Group B. Polysyllables   多音节

1. Zhōngguó   2. gāngcái   3. xīngqī   4. huángsè   5. qióngrén

6. mèngxiǎng   7. dōngfāng   8. chànggē 9. guāngmíng 10. qiángdà

D Circle the back nasal simple or compound vowel according to what you hear.

圈出所听到的韵母。

Example：If you hear "ang" please circle "ang" in the list → eng (ang) ong ing iong

1. iang eng uang ing ong   2. ang ueng ing iang uang

3. ong uang ang eng ing   4. ing eng uang ueng ang

5. ueng ing iong eng ang   6. ang iong iang ing eng

E Draw a line to link the initial consonant and the front/back nasal simple or compound vowel according to what you hear.

根据所听到的音节用线连接声母和韵母。

d	éng		zh	uāng
ch	āng		m	ǐn
h	óng		j	uàn
s	iàn		c	iǎng

F Fill in the blanks according to the syllables you hear and add tone marks on them.

根据所听到的音节填空并标上声调。

1. zh ____   2. g ____   3. r ____   4. j ____   5. d ____

6. ____ uang   7. ____ eng   8. ____ ing   9. ____ iong   10. ____ iang

G Write out the syllable with its tone mark according to what you hear.

写出所听到的音节并标上声调。

Group A. Monosyllables　单音节

1. _____   2. _____   3. _____   4. _____

Group B. Polysyllables　多音节

1. _____   2. _____   3. _____   4. _____

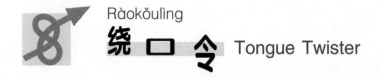

Ràokǒulìng
绕口令 Tongue Twister

Chuán hé Chuáng
船 和 床
A Boat and a Bed

Hǎi biān yǒu chuán,
海 边 有 船,

A boat is on the sea,

Chuán shang yǒu fān.
船 上 有 帆。

And there is a sail on it.

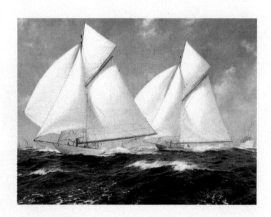

Fān yíngzhe fēng,
帆 迎着 风,

The sail is facing the wind,

Làng dǎzhe chuán.
浪 打着 船。

And the waves are striking the boat.

Chuán fānle shēn……
船 翻了 身……

Now the boat turned over...

Hǎi biān yǒu fáng,
海　边　有　房,
There is a cottage on the beach,

Fáng li yǒu chuáng.
房　里　有　床。
And there is a bed in it.

Chuáng shang tǎngzhe fānle chuán de rén.
床　　　上　　躺着 翻了　船　的　人。
The boatman is rescued and now is in the bed.

10

汉语音节

Chinese Syllables

第十课 汉语音节

这一课，我们先介绍汉语音节的拼写规则，然后讨论汉语双音节和多音节在发音时的变调规则。

拼写规则

1. 音节分隔规则

我们在第一课中提到，汉语音节通常由声母和韵母组成，然而，有些汉语音节也可以只有韵母而没有声母。例如，汉语音节"é"、"ī"和"ǘ"的意思可以分别代表"鹅"，"衣"和"鱼"。当一个音节没有声母而只含有一个韵母时，它可能会引起拼音书写上的混淆。例如，韵母"ā"和"í"可以是独立的两个音节表示"阿姨"。可是，"a"和"i"合成的"ài"本身也是一个音节，意思是"爱"。所以，为了避免这些零声母造成音节在拼音书写时的混淆，在汉语拼音里采用隔音字母"y"和"w"，还有隔音符号（'）来分隔易造成混淆的音节。

1）隔音字母"y"和"w"的用法

汉语拼音采用"y"和"w"做隔音字母是因为"y"和"w"在英语里都是半元音，"y"的发音接近汉语的单韵母"i"，"w"的发音接近汉语的单韵母"u"，所以用它们给以"i"打头和以"u"打头的零声母音节作隔音字母比较合适。"y"和"w"有它们的字母音，"y"读作"ia"，"w"读作"ua"。当它们作为隔音字母用于拼音中时，自然就成了韵母的一部分，于是"y"读作汉语单韵母音"i"，"w"读作汉语单韵母音"u"。

Lesson 10 Chinese Syllables

In this lesson we will first introduce the spelling rules for Chinese syllables and then discuss the rules of tone sandhi in pronouncing disyllables or polysyllables.

Spelling Rules

1. Rules for Syllable Separation

As mentioned in Lesson 1, Chinese syllables usually consist of initial consonants and simple or compound vowels. However, some Chinese syllables are composed of simple or compound vowels without initial consonant. For example, Chinese syllables "é", "ī", and "ǘ" represent *goose*, *clothes*, and *fish* respectively. When a syllable with zero initial consonant contains only a vowel, it could cause confusion in phonetic spelling. For example, the simple vowel "ā" and "í" can be used as separate syllables which together represent the word *aunt*. However, "ài" can be used as one syllable which represents the word *love*. In order to avoid confusion in phonetic spelling for those syllables with zero initial consonant, the separation letters "y" and "w" and the separation mark (') which is called apostrophe in English are used in Chinese phonetic spelling.

1) Usages of "y" and "w" as the Separation Letters

The reason for choosing "y" and "w" as the separation letters in Chinese phonetic spelling is that "y" and "w" both are semi-vowels in English. The pronunciation of "y" is close to the Chinese simple vowel "i" and "w" is close to the Chinese simple vowel "u". Thus it is relatively convenient to use them as the separation letters for zero initial consonant syllables beginning with "i" and "u". However, "y" and "w" have their own pronunciations. The prounciation of "y" is "ia" and the pronunciation of "w" is "ua". When they are used in Chinese *pinyin* as separation letters and become part of the vowel, "y" is pronounced the same as Chinese simple vowel "i" and "w" is pronounced the same as Chinese simple vowel "u".

"y" 和 "w" 的使用规则如下：

- 当 "i" 自身为一个音节时，在 "i" 之前加上 "y"，即：i → yi；当一个音节以 "i" 打头时，把 "i" 改写成 "y"（除了 "in" 和 "ing"），也就是：ia→ya, ie→ye, iao →yao, iou→you, ian→yan, iang→yang, iong →yong；当 "in" 和 "ing" 自身是音节时，在 "i" 之前加上 "y"，即：in → yin, ing → ying。

- 当 "u" 自身为一个音节时，在 "u" 之前加上 "w"，即：u → wu；当一个音节以 "u" 打头时，把 "u" 改写成 "w"，即：ua → wa, uo → wo, uai → wai, uei → wei, uan → wan, uen → wen, uang → wang, ueng → weng。

- 当 "ü" 自身为一个音节，或一个音节以 "ü" 打头时，在 "ü" 之前加上 "y"，同时去掉 ü 上面的两点，即：ü→yu, üe→yue, üan→yuan, ün → yun。

2）隔音符号（'）的用法

以 a, o, e 打头的零声母音节若跟随在以 "a" 或 "i" 为韵母的音节后面时，前后两个音节就需要用隔音符号（'）来分隔，于是，Xī ān（西安，中国的一个城市）一词正确的拼写应该是 Xī' ān，而 pí ǎo（皮袄）应该是 pí' ǎo。

此外，以 a, o, e 打头的零声母音节若跟随在以鼻音 "n" 或 "ng" 为结尾韵母的音节后面时，也需要用隔音符号（'）来分隔前后两个音节。例如：fáng ài（妨碍）应该写成 fáng' ài，而 dàng àn（档案）应该写成 dàng' àn。

Rules for Using "y" and "w" :

- When "i" itself is a syllable, add "y" before "i". That's, i→ yi; when a syllable begins with "i", change "i" into "y" (except "in" and "ing"). Thus, ia → ya, ie→ ye, iao→ yao, iou→you, ian→yan, iang→yang, and iong→yong. When "in" and "ing" are syllables by themselves, add "y" before "i". Thus, in → yin, ing → ying.

- When "u" is a syllable by itself, add "w" before "u". That is, u→wu. When a syllable begins with "u", change "u" into "w". Thus, ua→wa, uo→wo, uai→wai, uei→wei, uan→wan, uen→wen, uang→wang, and ueng→weng.

- When "ü" is a syllable by itself or when a syllable begins with "ü", add "y" before "ü" and remove the umlaut (the two dots) from "ü". Thus, ü→yu, üe→yue, üan→ yuan, and ün →yun.

2) Usages of the Separation Mark (')

When the zero initial consonant syllables beginning with a, o, e follow a vowel ending in "a" or "i", the use of a separation mark (') between the two syllables is required. Thus, the phonetic spelling for the word Xī ān (a city name of China) should be written as Xī'ān. And pí ǎo (fur-lined jacket) →pí'ǎo.

When syllables ended with nasals "n" or "ng" are followed by a zero initial consonant syllables beginning with a , o , e, the use of a separation mark is also required. For instance, a phonetic spelling word fáng ài (to hinder) should be written as fáng'ài. And dàng àn (files) →dàng'àn.

2. 省略规则

为了书写方便，拼音中运用了一些省略。

当声母 j, q, x 后面跟着韵母"ü"或是以"ü"打头的韵母时，"ü"上面的两点省略，即：jü → ju, jüe →jue, jüan → juan, jün → jun, qü → qu, qüe → que, qüan → quan, qün → qun, xü → xu, xüe → xue, xüan → xuan, xün → xun。原因是汉语中 j, q, x 不可能与"u"相拼，所以，去掉"ü"上面的两点并不会引起拼音书写的混淆。

iou, uei, uen 作为韵母跟别的声母相拼，写成 iu, ui, un。例如：niou→niu, guei→gui, lu-en→lun。这样省略的根据是，o、e 在某些条件下会发生丢音和弱化现象。所以，汉语拼音拼写规则为了统一形式便于实用，一律把声母后面的 iou, uei, uen 写成 iu, ui, un。

3. 声调标调规则

汉语拼音中声调是不可缺少的。声调总是标在韵母中的元音字母上，不能标在声母上。如果一个音节中只有一个元音，那么声调就标在这个元音上。如果一个音节中含有复韵母，那么声调标调遵循 a, o, e, i, u, ü 的次序，也就是说，如果一个音节含有"a"和其他元音，应把声调标在"a"上面；如果没有"a"，则把声调标在"o"上面，以此类推。不过，"ui"和"iu"是个例外，我们得把声调标在最后一个元音上，例如：liu → liú, dui → duì。

4. 双音节和多音节拼写规则

当我们用拼音拼写双音节和多音节时，我们应该遵守以下规则：

● 如果这些音节组成一个词，音节间不必有空格。例如：lǎo shī（老师）的拼写是 lǎoshī。

● 句子及专有名词的首字母需大写。例如：Zhōngguó（中国）。

● 移行要按音节分开，在没有写完的地方加上连字符号。例如：…………Lǎo-shī（老师），不能移作"Lǎ-oshī"。

2. Rules for Omission

For the sake of spelling convenience, a few omission rules are applied in phonetic spelling.

When the initial consonants j, q, x are followed by "ü" or a vowel which begins with "ü", remove the umlaut (the two dots) from "ü". That is, jü → ju, jüe→jue, jüan →juan, jün→jun, qü →qu, qüe→que, qüan→ quan, qün→qun, xü→ xu, xüe→ xue, xüan→ xuan and xün→ xun. Since j, q, x in Chinese never go with "u", the omission of umlaut from the "ü" will not cause confusion in phonetic spelling.

In addition, when "iou", "uei", "uen" go with the initial consonants, they are written as "iu", "ui", "un" respectively. For example, niou→niu, guei→gui, luen→lun. This rule is based on the fact that the sounds of "o" and "e" often get lost or weakened in some linguistic environments. For the sake of uniformity and function, "iou", "uei", "uen" after the initial consonants are always written as "iu", "ui" and "un".

3. Rules for Marking Tones

A tone mark is an indispensable part in Chinese *pinyin*. Tones are marked only on the vowel of each syllable and never on the initial consonants. If there is only one vowel in a syllable, mark the tone above that vowel. If there is a compound vowel in a syllable, tone mark assignment should follow the priority sequence of a, o, e, i, u and ü. That is, if a syllable contains an "a" and other vowels, place the tone mark on the top of "a". If there is no "a", then place the tone mark on the top of "o" and so on. However, there is an exception for "ui" and "iu", we always place the tone mark above the last vowel. Thus, liu → liú, and dui→ duì.

4. Rules for Spelling Disyllables or Polysyllables

When spelling disyllables or polysyllables, we should obey the following rules:

- Leave no space between the syllables if they form a word. For example, lǎo shī (teacher) is written as lǎoshī.

- Capitalize the first letter of a sentence or a proper noun. For example: Zhōngguó (China).

- If a word breaks at the end of a line, divide a word with a hyphen at a syllable ending at the end of the line. For example, ······ ······ ······ ······ ······ ······ ······ ······ ··· Lǎo-shī (teacher). "Lǎ-oshī" is wrong.

变调规则

前面我们已经提到，汉语是一种声调语言，根据音高来判断，汉语的每个音节都有不同的调值。对于一个独立的汉语音节来说，其调值是固定的。然而，在语流中，调值往往发生变化，一个汉语音节在语流中的调值是由语境决定的。汉语声调变化比较复杂，这里我们仅介绍几条基本的规则。

1. 轻声

我们在第五课中提到，轻声又可称为零声调。轻声音节在发音时应该轻且短。轻声可以发生在下面（但是不只限于）这些情况中：

- 在一些双音节词中，第二个音节应该读作轻声。例如：xiānsheng（先生），māma（妈妈），yìsi（意思）。

- 在一些三音节短语中，第二个音节应该读作轻声。例如：děng yi děng（等一等），shuō bu wán（说不完），shuō de hǎo（说得好）。

- 所有的助词应该读作轻声。例如：zǒu le（走了），tā de（他的/她的），hǎo ba（好吧）。

2. 第三声的变调

当两个第三声音节并列时，第一个第三声应该读成第二声。例如，nǐ hǎo 应该读成 ní hǎo。当三个第三声音节并列时，第一个第三声和第二个第三声都应该读成第二声。例如：

zhǎnlǎnguǎn（展览馆）应该读作 zhánlánguǎn

diǎn hǎo huǒ（点好火）应该读作 dián háo huǒ

jǔ qǐ shǒu（举起手）应该读作 jú qí shǒu

Rules for Tone Sandhi

We mentioned earlier that Chinese is a tonal language. Each syllable has a distinctive tone based on its pitch level. The tone pitch for a syllable is fixed when the syllable appears individually. However, the tone pitch for a syllable may change in spoken language, which brings about a change of tone of the syllable. Rules for tone sandhi in Chinese are complicated, so here we introduce only the very basic ones.

1. Neutral Tone

As mentioned in Lesson 5, the neutral tone is also referred as zero tone. The syllable with the neutral tone should be pronounced shortly and lightly. Neutral tones happen in (but are not limited to) the following situations:

- In some disyllabic words, the second syllable should be pronounced as the neutral tone, for example, xiānsheng (Mr.; Sir), māma (mother; mom), yìsi (meaning).

- In some trisyllabic phrases, the second syllable should be pronounced as the neutral tone. To cite a few examples: děng yi děng (wait a moment), shuō bu wán (speak endlessly) and shuō de hǎo (speak well).

- All auxiliary words are pronounced as neutral tones. For example, zǒu le (left), tā de (his/her) and hǎo ba (okay).

2. Tone Sandhi for the Third Tone

When two third tone syllables appear together, the first syllable changes to the second tone. For example, nǐ hǎo should be pronounced as ní hǎo. When three third tone syllables appear together, both the first and second syllables change to the second tone. Below are some examples:

zhǎnlǎnguǎn (exhibition hall) read as zhánlánguǎn

diǎn hǎo huǒ (lit a fire) read as dián háo huǒ

jǔ qǐ shǒu (raise your hand) read as jú qí shǒu

3. yī（一）和 bù（不）的变调

汉字"一"的基本声调是第一声"yī"，汉字"不"的基本声调是第四声"bù"，它们在下列情况下产生声调变化：

- 在双音节词中，如果 yī（一）后面是一个四声的音节，那么它应该读作第二声。例如：yíqiè（一切），yízhì（一致）。

- 在双音节或多音节词中，如果 yī（一）后面是一声、二声或三声的音节，那么它应该读作第四声。例如：yì tiān（一天），yì yán yì xíng（一言一行），yì běn（一本）。

- 在双音节词中，如果 bù（不）后面是一个四声的音节，那么它应该读作第二声。例如：bú yào（不要），bú qù（不去）。

- 在三音节短语中，如果 yī（一）或者 bù（不）是第二个音节，那么它们应该读作轻声。例如：xiǎng yi xiǎng（想一想），tīng yi tīng（听一听），hǎo bu hǎo（好不好），qù bu qù（去不去）。

3. Tone Sandhi for Words yī（一）**and** bù（不）

The basic tone for the Chinese character "一"（yī）is the first tone, and for "不"（bù）is the fourth tone, but their tones change in the following situations：

- In a disyllabic word, if yī is placed before a fourth tone syllable, it should be pronounced as the second tone, for example：yíqiè（everything）, yízhì（consistent）.

- In a disyllabic or polysyllabic word, if yī is placed before a non-fourth tone syllable（could be the first, second, or third tone）, it should be pronounced as the fourth tone, for example：yì tiān（a day）, yì yán yī xíng（words and deeds）, yì běn（one piece）.

- In a disyllabic word, if bù is placed before a fourth tone syllable, it should be read as the second tone, for example：bú yào（do not want; needn't）, bú qù（not to go）.

- In a trisyllabic phrase, if yī or bù is the second syllable, both of them are read as the neutral tone, for example：xiǎng yi xiǎng（have a think）, tīng yi tīng（have a listen）, hǎo bu hǎo（Is this ok?）and qù bu qù（To go or not?）.

Exercises 练习

A Read aloud the following syllables and pay attention to the spelling rules.

朗读下列音节，并注意拼音拼写规则。

1. u：kǔ — wǔ
2. i：mī — yī
3. ia：jiā — yā
4. ie：qiè — yè
5. ua：guà — wà
6. uo：huǒ — wǒ
7. üe：lüè — yuè
8. iao：tiào — yào
9. iou（iu）：liǔ — yǒu
10. uai：huài — wài
11. uei（ui）：suì — wèi
12. ün：jūn — yūn
13. ian：nián — yán
14. uan：huán — wán
15. üan：juǎn — yuǎn
16. uen（un）：gùn — wèn
17. ing：píng — yíng
18. iang：liáng — yáng
19. uang：huàng — wàng
20. iong：jiǒng — yǒng
21. ueng：wēng

B Read aloud the following syllables.

朗读下列音节。

1. iou（iu）：xiū — jiū — qiú — liú
2. uei（ui）：huí — tuī — zuì — shuǐ
3. uen（un）：dūn — chún — kùn — lùn
4. ü（u）：xū — qù — jǔ — yǔ

C Read aloud the following syllables and pay attention to the separation mark.

朗读下列音节并注意隔音符号。

1. nǚ'ér（daughter）
2. xǐ'ài（to like）
3. Xī'ān（name of a city）
4. shí'èr（twelve）
5. Cháng'é（name of a person）
6. fáng'ài（to hinder）

D Read aloud the following syllables and pay attention to the neutral tone.

朗读下列音节并注意轻声。

1. māma
2. bàba
3. jiějie
4. chúle
5. bízi
6. nǐmen
7. bōli
8. dòufu
9. juéde
10. piányi

E Read aloud the following underlined words and pay attention to the tone sandhis.

朗读下列画线的词并注意声调变化。

Group A

1. nǐ hǎo → ní hǎo   2. chǐrǔ → chírǔ   3. qǔshě → qúshě

4. xǐ zǎo → xí zǎo   5. liǎojiě → liáojiě   6. wǔdǎo → wúdǎo

7. qǐpǎo → qípǎo   8. biǎoyǎnzhě → biáoyǎnzhě

9. dǎnxiǎoguǐ → dánxiáoguǐ   10. bǎibǎi shǒu → báibái shǒu

Group B

1. 一 (yī)

   yìqǐ   yìbiān   yìxiē   yì kǒu   yíqiè   yígài   yízhì   yídào

2. 不 (bù)

   búcuò   bú duì   bú shì   búdàn   bù xíng   bùjiǔ   bù dǒng   bùguǎn

F Add tone marks to the following syllables according to what you hear.

根据所听到的音节标调。

1. hai   2. lao   3. mei   4. zhuan   5. qiang

6. gun   7. miao   8. niu   9. dui   10. lüe

11. shuang   12. jun   13. hua   14. kou   15. jin

16. chang   17. weng   18. duo   19. ben   20. pan

G Write out the syllable with its tone mark according to what you hear.

写出所听到的音节并标上声调。

Group A. Monosyllables   单音节

1. _____   2. _____   3. _____   4. _____   5. _____

6. _____   7. _____   8. _____   9. _____   10. _____

Group B. Polysyllables   多音节

1. _____   2. _____   3. _____   4. _____   5. _____

6. _____   7. _____   8. _____   9. _____   10. _____

11. _____   12. _____

Shīgē
诗歌 Poem

Jìng Yè Sī
静 夜 思

Night Thoughts

Táng　　　Lǐ Bái
唐　·　李 白

Tang Dynasty · Li Bai

Chuáng qián míng yuèguāng,
床　　前　明　　月光,

Before my bed, the moon is shining bright,

Yí shì dì shang shuāng.
疑　是　地　上　　霜。

like frost spreading on the ground.

Jǔ tóu wàng míng yuè,
举　头　望　　明　　月,

I raise my head and look at the bright moon,

Dī tóu sī gùxiāng.
低　头　思　故乡。

I lower my head and think of home.

A 附 录
Appendix

Useful Classroom Expressions 课堂教学常用语

Lesson 2   第二课

C.

1. a   2. o   3. e   4. i   5. u   6. ü   7. b   8. p   9. m   10. f

D.

1. er e ⓞ u a   2. i ⓤ a f ü   3. b p ⓜ o u

4. a u f b ⓔ   5. f o i ⓤ u   6. e a ⓘ f b

E.

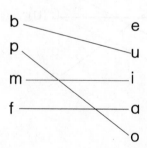

b   e

p   u

m   i

f   a

         o

F.

1. b<u>o</u>   2. p<u>a</u>   3. mi   4. f<u>u</u>   5. <u>b</u>a   6. pi   7. <u>m</u>o   8. <u>f</u>a

G.

Group A

1. u   2. ü   3. i   4. e   5. f   6. m   7. a   8. er   9. p   10. o

Group B

1. fa   2. mo   3. bu   4. po   5. bi   6. ba   7. mi   8. fu   9. pi   10. mu

Lesson 3 第三课

C.

1. d   2. t   3. n   4. l   5. g

6. k   7. h   8. j   9. q   10. x

D.

1. l ⓖ h t n   2. d h n ⓚ g   3. j ⓠ x t h

4. h t l g ⓓ   5. x q ⓙ t d   6. t n h ⓧ q

E.

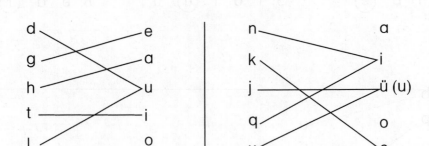

F.

1. la̲   2. ge̲   3. te̲   4. ni̲   5. qi̲   6. xu̲   7. h̲e   8. ju

G.

Group A

1. n   2. j   3. t   4. x   5. h

6. l   7. e   8. i   9. q   10. d

Group B

1. ga   2. ku   3. xu   4. ji   5. qu

6. le   7. po   8. bu   9. nü   10. te

Lesson 4　第四课

C.

1. z　2. c　3. s　4. zh　5. ch

6. sh　7. r　8. j　9. q　10. x

D.

1. r (sh) s z zh　2. zh r (z) c s　3. ch (c) r sh z

4. sh c s (ch) r　5. c ch (s) sh zh　6. sh ch (r) zh ch

E.

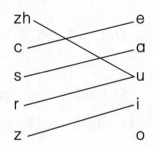
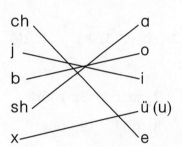

F.

1. r<u>e</u>　2. ch<u>u</u>　3. s<u>e</u>　4. zh<u>a</u>　5. <u>ch</u>i　6. <u>z</u>a　7. <u>she</u>　8. <u>z</u>u

G.

Group A

1. ch　2. z　3. sh　4. r　5. zh　6. s　7. g　8. h　9. t　10. j

Group B

1. sha　2. chu　3. zu　4. si　5. ru　6. zhe

7. he　8. qu　9. da　10. lü　11. ge　12. bo

Lesson 5   第五课

C.

1. gē gé gě ⓖè   2. qū qú ⓠǔ qù   3. ⓒī cí cǐ cì

4. mō ⓜó mǒ mò   5. shā shá shǎ ⓢhà   6. zū zú ⓩǔ zù

D.

1. qūzhé   2. dàdì   3. pífū   4. dúlì   5. nàlǐ

6. zhùzhǐ   7. shīgē   8. rìchū   9. tímù   10. zìjù

E.

Group A

1. kè   2. shì   3. kǔ   4. dé   5. pō   6. zhú   7. sà   8. xū

Group B

1. zhèlǐ   2. jìxù   3. zhǔxí   4. kěshì   5. fādá   6. lìqì

7. lǜshī   8. nàlǐ   9. pǔjí   10. tūchū   11. dìzhǐ   12. fùzá

Lesson 6　第六课

D.

1. ia (ie) ua ao üe　　2. ao (ou) ua uo ai　　3. ia (ai) ou ua ie

4. ua ei ou ie (uo)　　5. üe ei (ao) ua ia　　6. ai ao (ia) ie ua

E.

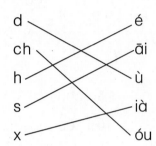

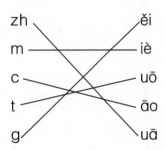

F.

1. zh<u>à</u>o　　2. g<u>ō</u>u　　3. r<u>uò</u>　　4. j<u>ué</u>　　5. c<u>ài</u>

6. l<u>iè</u>　　7. <u>h</u>uā　　8. <u>f</u>ēi　　9. <u>z</u>ài　　10. <u>d</u>ōu

G.

Group A

1. hǎo　　2. mài　　3. suō　　4. lòu

5. qiè　　6. jiǎ　　7. zài　　8. huà

Group B

1. xǔnuò　　2. kāishǐ　　3. féiròu　　4. lǐjiě　　5. lǎohǔ

6. chǎojià　　7. guòqù　　8. xuéxí　　9. hēisè　　10. xiàkè

Lesson 7 第七课

D.

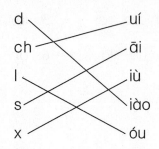

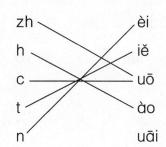

E.

1. xi<u>à</u>o   2. j<u>iū</u>   3. z<u>uì</u>   4. h<u>uài</u>   5. ch<u>uí</u>

6. <u>l</u>ào   7. <u>m</u>ài   8. <u>sh</u>uǐ   9. <u>li</u>ú   10. <u>z</u>ǎo

F.

Group A

1. biǎo   2. kuài   3. suī   4. xiū

5. ruǐ   6. jiǎo   7. huī   8. gài

Group B

1. liǎojiě   2. shuìjiào   3. lánqiú   4. qíguài   5. jiàoshì

6. huíjiā   7. xiū jià   8. mǎi piào   9. guāiqiǎo   10. cháoxiào

Lesson 8   第八课

D.

1. ian en uan (in) üan   2. an (un) in ian uan   3. ian uan un (ün) en

4. un en uan üan (an)   5. ün un in (en) an   6. an (in) ian üan un

E.

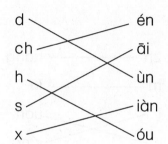 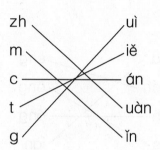

F.

1. zhàn   2. guān   3. rén   4. juǎn   5. suàn

6. lán   7. huān   8. fēn   9. dùn   10. tiān

G.

Group A

1. miàn   2. sūn   3. gēn   4. huán

Group B

1. lǐlùn   2. hùnluàn   3. chī fàn   4. niánjí

Lesson 9　第九课

D.

1. iang ⊙eng uang ing ong　　2. ang ueng ing iang ⊙uang

3. ong uang ang eng ⊙ing　　4. ing eng uang ⊙ueng ang

5. ueng ing ⊙iong eng ang　　6. ang iong ⊙iang ing eng

E.

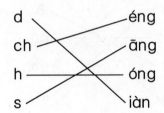
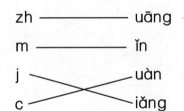

F.

1. <u>zh</u>āng　2. <u>gu</u>ǎng　3. <u>r</u>ēng　4. <u>j</u>iǒng　5. <u>d</u>īng

6. <u>k</u>uàng　7. <u>f</u>ēng　8. <u>q</u>ǐng　9. <u>x</u>ióng　10. <u>x</u>iǎng

G.

Group A

1. liàng　　2. nóng　　3. xǐng　　4. téng

Group B

1. fēicháng　2. jiānglái　　3. juédìng　　4. zhèngzài

Lesson 10　第十课

F.

1. hǎi	2. lāo	3. měi	4. zhuàn	5. qiǎng
6. gùn	7. miáo	8. niù	9. duī	10. lüè
11. shuāng	12. jùn	13. huá	14. kǒu	15. jīn
16. cháng	17. wēng	18. duǒ	19. bèn	20. pán

G.

Group A

1. mǎo	2. liàng	3. xūn	4. duǎn	5. yún
6. jìn	7. wēn	8. zhōu	9. kāng	10. huáng

Group B

1. xuésheng	2. qiūtiān	3. diànyǐng	4. xīwàng
5. dì'èr	6. wǒmen	7. wǎnhuì	8. yóuyǒng
9. Běijīng	10. Tiānjīn	11. Shànghǎi	12. Chóngqìng

R参考文献
eferences

Chao, Y-R. (1933). Tone and intonation in Chinese. *Academic Sinica*：*Bulletin of the Institute of History and Philology*, 4：121-134.

Duanmu, S. (2000). *The Phonology of the World's Languages*. New York：Oxford University Press.

Ramsey, S. R. (1987). *The Language of* China. Princeton, NJ：Princeton University Press.

Stimson, H. M. (1975). *Introduction to Chinese Pronunciation and the Pinyin Romanization*. New Haven, Connecticut：Far Eastern Publications, Yale University.

黄伯荣、廖序东主编（1981），现代汉语，兰州：甘肃人民出版社。

黄政澄主编（1998），标准汉语教程，北京：北京大学出版社。

吴洁敏（1992），汉英语音对比分析（224－237），选自中国对外汉语教学学会华东地区协作组主编《面向世界的汉语教学》，上海：复旦大学出版社。

邵敬敏主编（2001），现代汉语通论，上海：上海教育出版社。

汉语大字典（第二版，1995），武汉：四川辞书出版社。

www. chinese-poems. com

Acknowledgments

The lead author of this textbook, Helen H. Shen, would like to thank the Center for Asian and Pacific Studies at the University of Iowa, USA for awarding a Research Grant to support this textbook project. She also would like to express her heartfelt appreciation to HoJung Choi for assisting in image design and Kimela Nelson, Lois Muehl for English editing.

鸣　谢

本书的主要作者 Helen H. Shen 向爱荷华大学亚洲太平洋研究中心表示感谢！该中心提供的研究基金使作者能及时完成本书的写作。

HoJung Choi 为本书设计了插图，Kimela Nelson 和 Lois Muehl 对本教材的英文文本作了细致的校对。在此，一并表示诚挚的谢意。

本书配套CD目录
The Contents of the Supporting CD of the Textbook

中文编辑：王　轩
　　　　　周婉梅
英文编辑：武思敏
装帧设计：苏芳蕾

ISBN 978-7-5619-1618-6

全套定价：52.00元
（含课本及录音CD、练习册及录音MP3）

海外视角汉语教材
A Chinese Textbook from Overseas Perspectives

汉语拼音入门
Hànyǔ Pīnyīn Rùmén

练习册
Liànxícè

编著：

Helen H. Shen

Chen-Hui Tsai   Yunong Zhou

Introduction to Standard Chinese *Pinyin* System
Workbook

北京语言大学出版社
BEIJING LANGUAGE AND CULTURE
UNIVERSITY PRESS

海外视角汉语教材
A Chinese Textbook from Overseas Perspectives

Hànyǔ Pīnyīn Rùmén

Liànxícè

编著：
Helen H. Shen
Chen-Hui Tsai   Yunong Zhou

Introduction to Standard Chinese *Pinyin* System

Workbook

北京语言大学出版社
BEIJING LANGUAGE AND CULTURE
UNIVERSITY PRESS

Contents

目 录

How to Use the Workbook

This workbook consists of *Pinyin* exercises from Lesson 2 to Lesson 10, being strictly in line with the contents of the textbook. The aim is to help the beginners review and reinforce what they have learned in class. Each lesson consists of a cover and around 5 pages of *Pinyin* exercises. The *Pinyin* exercises begins with a warm-up which is followed by a variety of tasks. In each part, instructions are provided in the workbook itself as well as on the supporting CD. The ◁୬ sign indicates the corresponding sound recording on the CD. Please follow the instructions to find the corresponding recording file; then complete the task based on what you hear on the CD. All the sound clips are in mp3 format. An mp3 player is necessary for completing the exercises in the workbook. After completion of each lesson, please detach the entire lesson including the cover and submit it to the instructor. An answer key can be found in the back of the workbook for your reference.

The Characteristics of the Workbook

Most of the syllables presented in the workbook are the ones that are to be learned in the first-year Chinese class in overseas universities. In addition, other compound syllables that have been learned are also included. Therefore through practice, students can not only learn and master the *Pinyin* system, but also have an effective preview of the syllables of Chinese characters that are to be learned. This workbook helps learners master the *Pinyin* system in each unit in a step-by-step way (see the graph below).

Warm-up activity:
　　Review the target *Pinyin* items for the present lesson.

Individual exercise:
　　Target *Pinyin* items of the lesson are presented individually to reinforce the beginner's perception of individual *Pinyin* sounds.

Syllable exercise, stage Ⅰ:
　　In the exercises of this stage the learners should familiarize themselves with syllable pronunciation, with hints provided.

Syllable exercise, stage Ⅱ:
　　In the exercises of this stage the learners are required to provide one of the inital consonants of Chinese syllables and the simple or compound vowels according to the recording phonetic sound.

Syllable exercise, stage Ⅲ:
　　In this stage, the learners should be able to identify both the initial consonants and the simple or compound vowels in the syllables.

　　Besides this workbook, we have also established a website (http://www. uiowa. edu/~chinese) which provides interactive activities to help learners do focused exercises about the initial consonants of Chinese syllables and the simple or compound vowels that are easily confused. In this way, learners can review the content of the textbook more effectively.

~ Have fun with *Hanyu Pinyin*! ~

使用指南

　　《汉语拼音入门　练习册》紧密配合课本内容，涵盖了《汉语拼音入门》课本第二课到第十课的拼音练习，可以让学生对学过的拼音进行进一步复习和强化提高。练习册的每一课大多有五页拼音练习加上一页封面，以方便交作业。练习步骤由热身活动开始，先帮助学生回顾课堂讲授的重点，再开展多层次的练习，巩固所学的拼音知识。每一道题在练习册及配套光盘中都有详细的答题说明。声音图标◀)) 代表答题所需的录音，请依照题目的指示，找到相对应的录音文件。光盘内的录音皆为 MP3 格式，请使用 MP3 播放器来完成指定的练习任务。在完成每一课的拼音练习之后，请连同封面将整课的练习撕下，以便于老师批改。练习册最后附有参考答案，便于自学者使用。

《汉语拼音入门　练习册》特点介绍

　　在练习音节的选择上，本练习册主要以海外大学一年级中文课将学到的音节为主，再扩充至包含所学拼音的其他复合音节，因此在练习过程中，学生不仅是学习汉语拼音，还能对即将学习的汉语音节作有效的重点预习。本练习册的特点是通过由收到放、循序渐进的复习活动，使学生能逐步巩固每个单元的拼音知识，练习主要流程如下图所示。

热身活动：

复习教师在课堂上讲授的新内容。

声、韵母单独练习：

让学习者辨识单独的声母或韵母，强化他们对每一个声母、韵母的发音认知。

第一阶段音节练习：

这一阶段的练习，是在有提示的情况下，帮助学习者熟悉声、韵母的拼合发音。

第二阶段音节练习：

这个阶段的练习，让学习者根据所给的音提供音节中的其中一个声母或韵母。

第三阶段音节练习：

在这一阶段，学习者应能正确地辨听音节中的声母和韵母。

除了这本练习册外，我们还为本教材设了一个《汉语拼音入门》网站，提供在线互动练习，对容易混淆的声母和韵母进行重点训练，帮助学习者更有效地复习课本内容。请访问 http://www.uiowa.edu/~chinese。

祝愿大家都能快乐并成功地学习汉语拼音！

汉语拼音入门　练习册

Introduction to Standard Chinese *Pinyin* System
Workbook

2

Name : _____

Class : _____ Year : _____

 **Warm-up**

Please listen to the recording for a review of the simple vowels and initial consonants learned in class.

热身活动：请听录音，复习课上所学的单韵母和声母。

Simple Vowels 单韵母

1	2	3	4	5	6	7
a	o	e	er	i	u	ü
啊（ā）	哦（ò）	鹅（é）	耳（ěr）	衣（yī）	屋（wū）	鱼（yú）
ah！	oh！	goose	ear	clothes	house	fish

Initial Consonants 声母

1	2	3	4
b	p	m	f
波（bō）	坡（pō）	墨（mò）	佛（fó）
wave	slope	ink	Buddha

▶Part 1

Please listen to the recording and draw a line to link each picture with its corresponding simple vowel or initial consonant respectively. （11 points）

请听录音，将图片与相对应的韵母/声母用线连起来。

Simple Vowels 单韵母

1	2	3	4	5	6	7
●	●	●	●	●	●	●
●	●	●	●	●	●	●
a	i	e	ü	er	u	o

Initial Consonants 声母

1	2	3	4
●	●	●	●
●	●	●	●
p	b	f	m

▶ Part 2

Circle the simple vowel or initial consonant you hear. （10 points）

圈出所听到的声母或韵母。

1. 🔊   e   o   a

2. 🔊   ü   i   u

3. 🔊   er   i   ü

4. 🔊   e   er   u

5. 🔊   u   e   i

6. 🔊   a   o   u

7. 🔊   e   a   ü

8. 🔊   b   m   p

9. 🔊   m   f   p

10. 🔊   b   m   f

▶ Part 3

Please listen to the recording carefully, choose the correct one that matches the given simple vowel or initial consonant and fill its corresponding number in the bracket. (5 points)

请注意听录音，选出与所给声母或韵母一致的答案，把序号填在括号里。

1. o (   )   (1) 🔊   (2) 🔊   (3) 🔊

2. u (   )   (1) 🔊   (2) 🔊   (3) 🔊

3. e (   )   (1) 🔊   (2) 🔊   (3) 🔊

4. i (   )   (1) 🔊   (2) 🔊   (3) 🔊

5. b (   )   (1) 🔊   (2) 🔊   (3) 🔊

▶ Part 4

Please listen to the following syllables, choose the correct initial consonant and fill in the blank. (5 points)

请听下面的音节，选出正确的声母填在空格里。

1. 🔊   ＿＿a   (p   b)

2. 🔊   ＿＿o   (m   f)

3. 🔊   ＿＿i   (p   m)

4. 🔊   ＿＿u   (m   b)

5. 🔊   ＿＿u   (b   f)

▶ **Part 5**

Please listen to the following syllables and write out the missing initial consonant. (5 points)

请听下面的音节，并一一写出声母。

1. 🔊 ____ i   2. 🔊 ____ a   3. 🔊 ____ o

4. 🔊 ____ u   5. 🔊 ____ a

▶ **Part 6**

Please listen to the following syllables，choose the correct simple vowel and fill in the blank. (10 points)

请听下面的音节，选出正确的韵母填在空格里。

1. 🔊 b ____   (a   o)   2. 🔊 b ____   (i   u)

3. 🔊 b ____   (a   i)   4. 🔊 p ____   (a   o)

5. 🔊 p ____   (i   u)   6. 🔊 p ____   (i   a)

7. 🔊 m ____   (o   u)   8. 🔊 m ____   (i   u)

9. 🔊 m ____   (a   o)   10. 🔊 f ____   (a   u)

▶ **Part 7**

Please listen to the following syllables and write out the missing simple vowel. (20 points)

请听下面的音节，并一一写出韵母。

1. 🔊 p ____   2. 🔊 b ____   3. 🔊 m ____   4. 🔊 f ____   5. 🔊 p ____

6. 🔊 b ____   7. 🔊 m ____   8. 🔊 f ____   9. 🔊 p ____   10. 🔊 b ____

▶ Part 8

Please listen to the recording and write down the syllable according to what you hear.
(34 points)

请听录音，写出所听到的音节。

1. 🔊 _____

2. 🔊 _____

3. 🔊 _____

4. 🔊 _____

5. 🔊 _____

6. 🔊 _____

7. 🔊 _____

8. 🔊 _____

9. 🔊 _____

10. 🔊 _____

11. 🔊 _____

12. 🔊 _____

13. 🔊 _____

14. 🔊 _____

15. 🔊 _____

16. 🔊 _____

17. 🔊 _____

āéīōǔ

汉语拼音入门　练习册

Introduction to Standard Chinese *Pinyin* System
Workbook

3

Name : _____

Class : _____ Year : _____

▲Warm-up

Please listen to the recording for a review of the initial consonants learned in class.

热身活动：请听录音，复习课上所学的声母。

Initial Consonants 声母

1	2	3	4	5
d	t	n	l	g
得（dé）	特（tè）	那（nà）	乐（lè）	鸽（gē）
get	special	that	happy	dove

6	7	8	9	10
k	h	j	q	x
窠（kē）	喝（hē）	鸡（jī）	七（qī）	西（xī）
nest	drink	rooster	seven	west

Part 1

Please listen to the recording and draw a line to link each picture with its corresponding initial consonant respectively. (10 points)

请听录音，将图片与相对应的声母用线连起来。

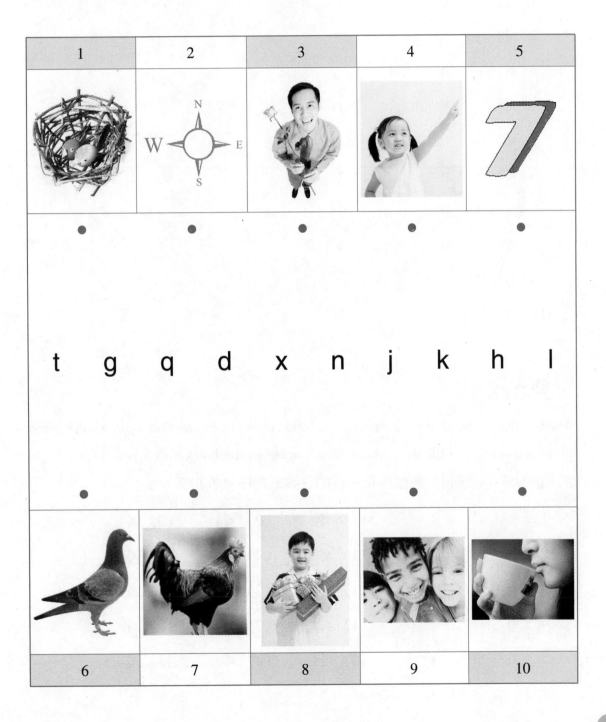

▶ Part 2

Circle the initial consonant you hear（10 points）

圈出所听到的声母。

1. 🔊　　d　　　t　　　l

2. 🔊　　n　　　l　　　k

3. 🔊　　h　　　k　　　g

4. 🔊　　k　　　j　　　h

5. 🔊　　j　　　x　　　q

6. 🔊　　n　　　d　　　t

7. 🔊　　n　　　g　　　l

8. 🔊　　h　　　g　　　k

9. 🔊　　j　　　q　　　x

10. 🔊　　x　　　j　　　h

▶ Part 3

Please listen to the recording carefully, choose the correct one that matches the given initial consonant and fill its corresponding number in the bracket.（5 points）

请注意听录音，选出与所给声母一致的答案，把序号填在括号里。

1. x　（　　）　　　（1）🔊　　（2）🔊　　（3）🔊

2. n　（　　）　　　（1）🔊　　（2）🔊　　（3）🔊

3. j　（　　）　　　（1）🔊　　（2）🔊　　（3）🔊

4. g　（　　）　　　（1）🔊　　（2）🔊　　（3）🔊

5. q　（　　）　　　（1）🔊　　（2）🔊　　（3）🔊

Part 4

For each question, please listen to the three sounds carefully and circle the one which does NOT share the same initial consonant with the other two. (5 points)

每道题有三个选项，其中有两个选项的声母是一样的，请注意听录音，把声母不同的选项圈起来。

1.　(1) 🔊　　(2) 🔊　　(3) 🔊

2.　(1) 🔊　　(2) 🔊　　(3) 🔊

3.　(1) 🔊　　(2) 🔊　　(3) 🔊

4.　(1) 🔊　　(2) 🔊　　(3) 🔊

5.　(1) 🔊　　(2) 🔊　　(3) 🔊

Part 5

Please listen to the following syllables, choose the correct initial consonant and fill in the blank. (10 points)

请听下面的音节，选出正确的声母填在空格里。

1. 🔊　＿＿a　　　（d　　t）

2. 🔊　＿＿u　　　（n　　l）

3. 🔊　＿＿e　　　（g　　k）

4. 🔊　＿＿i　　　（j　　q）

5. 🔊　＿＿i　　　（q　　x）

6. 🔊　＿＿ü　　　（x　　q）

7. 🔊　＿＿i　　　（q　　j）

8. 🔊　＿＿u　　　（g　　k）

9. 🔊　＿＿a　　　（n　　l）

10. 🔊　＿＿u　　　（d　　t）

▶ Part 6

Please listen to the following syllables and write out the missing initial consonant. (10 points)

请听下面的音节，并一一写出声母。

1. 🔊 ___i 2. 🔊 ___i 3. 🔊 ___u 4. 🔊 ___ü 5. 🔊 ___u

6. 🔊 ___a 7. 🔊 ___ü 8. 🔊 ___a 9. 🔊 ___i 10. 🔊 ___ü

▶ Part 7

Please listen to the recording and write down the syllable according to what you hear. (50 points)

请听录音，写出所听到的音节。

1. 🔊 _____   2. 🔊 _____   3. 🔊 _____

4. 🔊 _____   5. 🔊 _____   6. 🔊 _____

7. 🔊 _____   8. 🔊 _____   9. 🔊 _____

10. 🔊 _____   11. 🔊 _____   12. 🔊 _____

13. 🔊 _____   14. 🔊 _____   15. 🔊 _____

16. 🔊 _____   17. 🔊 _____   18. 🔊 _____

19. 🔊 _____   20. 🔊 _____   21. 🔊 _____

22. 🔊 _____   23. 🔊 _____   24. 🔊 _____

25. 🔊 _____

汉语拼音入门　练习册

Introduction to Standard Chinese *Pinyin* System

Workbook

4

Name : _____

Class : _____ Year : _____

📖 Warm-up

Please listen to the recording for a review of the initial consonants learned in class.

热身活动：请听录音，复习课上所学的声母。

Initial Consonants 声母

1	2	3
z	c	s
子（zǐ）	瓷（cí）	寺（sì）
son	porcelain	temple

4	5	6	7
zh	ch	sh	r
指（zhǐ）	齿（chǐ）	矢（shǐ）	日（rì）
finger	tooth	arrow	sun

Part 1

Please listen to the recording and draw a line to link each picture with its corresponding initial consonant respectively. （7 points）

请听录音，将图片与相对应的声母用线连起来。

1	2	3	4	5	6	7
●	●	●	●	●	●	●
●	●	●	●	●	●	●
z	r	zh	c	ch	s	sh

Part 2

Circle the initial consonant you hear. （10 points）

圈出所听到的声母。

1. 🔊　　z　　r　　sh

2. 🔊　　zh　　ch　　r

3. 🔊　　z　　zh　　ch

4. 🔊　　ch　　z　　c

5. 🔊 　　　sh　　　s　　　r

6. 🔊 　　　c　　　ch　　　z

7. 🔊 　　　z　　　sh　　　s

8. 🔊 　　　c　　　j　　　x

9. 🔊 　　　q　　　z　　　s

10. 🔊 　　　ch　　　s　　　sh

Part 3

Please listen to the recording carefully, choose the correct one that matches the given initial consonant and fill its corresponding number in the bracket. (10 points)

请注意听录音，选出与所给声母一致的答案，把序号填在括号里。

1. zh 　（　　）　　　（1）🔊　　　（2）🔊　　　（3）🔊

2. sh 　（　　）　　　（1）🔊　　　（2）🔊　　　（3）🔊

3. ch 　（　　）　　　（1）🔊　　　（2）🔊　　　（3）🔊

4. c 　　（　　）　　　（1）🔊　　　（2）🔊　　　（3）🔊

5. r 　　（　　）　　　（1）🔊　　　（2）🔊　　　（3）🔊

Part 4

For each question, please listen to the three sounds carefully and circle the one which does NOT share the same initial consonant with the other two. (10 points)

每道题有三个选项，其中有两个选项的声母是一样的，请注意听录音，把声母不同的选项圈起来。

1. 　（1）🔊　　　（2）🔊　　　（3）🔊

2. 　（1）🔊　　　（2）🔊　　　（3）🔊

3. 　（1）🔊　　　（2）🔊　　　（3）🔊

4.　（1）🔊　　（2）🔊　　（3）🔊

5.　（1）🔊　　（2）🔊　　（3）🔊

▶Part 5

Please listen to the following syllables，choose the correct initial consonant and fill in the blank.（10 points）

请听下面的音节，选出正确的声母填在空格里。

1.　🔊　____ a　　　　（c　　　r）

2.　🔊　____ u　　　　（sh　　s）

3.　🔊　____ e　　　　（c　　ch）

4.　🔊　____ i　　　　（s　　　z）

5.　🔊　____ i　　　　（s　　　c）

6.　🔊　____ a　　　　（ch　sh）

7.　🔊　____ i　　　　（sh　　r）

8.　🔊　____ u　　　　（zh　ch）

9.　🔊　____ e　　　　（sh　　r）

10.　🔊　____ e　　　　（s　　　z）

▶Part 6

Please listen to the following syllables and write out the missing initial consonant.（7 points）

请听下面的音节，并一一写出声母。

1. 🔊 ____ i　　2. 🔊 ____ i　　3. 🔊 ____ u

4. 🔊 ____ a　　5. 🔊 ____ u　　6. 🔊 ____ i

7. 🔊 ____ e

▶ Part 7

Please listen to the recording and write down the syllable according to what you hear.
（46 points）

请听录音，写出所听到的音节。

1. 🔊 _____   2. 🔊 _____   3. 🔊 _____

4. 🔊 _____   5. 🔊 _____   6. 🔊 _____

7. 🔊 _____   8. 🔊 _____   9. 🔊 _____

10. 🔊 _____   11. 🔊 _____   12. 🔊 _____

13. 🔊 _____   14. 🔊 _____   15. 🔊 _____

16. 🔊 _____   17. 🔊 _____   18. 🔊 _____

19. 🔊 _____   20. 🔊 _____   21. 🔊 _____

22. 🔊 _____   23. 🔊 _____

汉语拼音入门　练习册

Introduction to Standard Chinese *Pinyin* System

Workbook

5

Name : _____

Class : _____ Year : _____

🔊Warm-up

Please listen to the recording for a review of the tones learned in class.

热身活动：请听录音，复习课上所学的声调。

Tones　声调

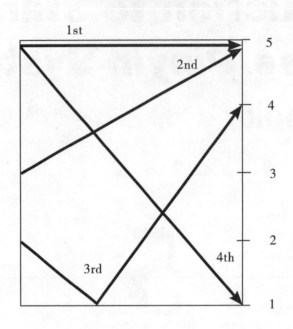

1	2	3	4
mā	má	mǎ	mà
妈	麻	马	骂
mother	linen	horse	to scold

Part 1

Please listen to the recording and draw a line to link each picture with its corresponding tone. (4 points)

请听录音，将图片与相对应的声调用线连起来。

1	2	3	4

●	●	●	●
●	●	●	●
mā	mà	má	mǎ

Part 2

Circle the tone you hear. (10 points)

圈出所听到的声调。

1. 🔊   gē   gé   gě   gè

2. 🔊   dā   dá   dǎ   dà

3. 🔊   chū   chú   chǔ   chù

23

4. 🔊　　　nā　　　ná　　　nǎ　　　nà

5. 🔊　　　shī　　　shí　　　shǐ　　　shì

6. 🔊　　　qī　　　qí　　　qǐ　　　qì

7. 🔊　　　kē　　　ké　　　kě　　　kè

8. 🔊　　　lī　　　lí　　　lǐ　　　lì

9. 🔊　　　fū　　　fú　　　fǔ　　　fù

10. 🔊　　　yū　　　yú　　　yǔ　　　yù

▶Part 3

Please listen to the recording carefully, choose the correct one that has the same tone with the given syllable and fill its corresponding number in the bracket. (5 points)

请注意听录音，选出与所给音节声调一致的答案，把序号填在括号里。

1. zhī　　（　　）　　　（1）🔊　　（2）🔊　　（3）🔊

2. hé　　（　　）　　　（1）🔊　　（2）🔊　　（3）🔊

3. mǐ　　（　　）　　　（1）🔊　　（2）🔊　　（3）🔊

4. sù　　（　　）　　　（1）🔊　　（2）🔊　　（3）🔊

5. bí　　（　　）　　　（1）🔊　　（2）🔊　　（3）🔊

▶Part 4

For each question, please listen to the three tones carefully and circle the one which does NOT share the same tone with the other two. (5 points)

每道题有三个选项，其中有两个选项的声调是一样的，请注意听录音，把声调不同的选项圈起来。

1.　（1）🔊　　　　（2）🔊　　　　（3）🔊

2.　（1）🔊　　　　（2）🔊　　　　（3）🔊

3.   (1) 🔊   (2) 🔊   (3) 🔊
4.   (1) 🔊   (2) 🔊   (3) 🔊
5.   (1) 🔊   (2) 🔊   (3) 🔊

▶ Part 5

Please listen to the recording and circle the correct tone according to what you hear. （9 points）

请听录音，圈出所听到的声调。

1. 🔊 zi   （ −   ＼ ）

2. 🔊 qi   （ −   ／ ）

3. 🔊 he   （ ／   ＼ ）

4. 🔊 mu   （ −   ＼ ）

5. 🔊 wo   （ −   ˅ ）

6. 🔊 ji   （ −   ／ ）

7. 🔊 ba   （ ˅   ＼ ）

8. 🔊 ru   （ ˅   ／ ）

9. 🔊 qu   （ ／   ＼ ）

▶ Part 6

Please listen to the recording and add tone marks to the following syllables. （10 points）
请听录音，为下面的音节标上声调。

1. 🔊 li   2. 🔊 ba   3. 🔊 pu   4. 🔊 e   5. 🔊 si

6. 🔊 de   7. 🔊 sa   8. 🔊 lü   9. 🔊 ne   10. 🔊 tu

▶Part 7

Please listen to the recording and write down the syllable with its tone mark according to what you hear.（57 points）

请听录音，写出所听到的音节并标上声调。

A. Monosyllables（45 points） 单音节

1. 🔊 _____   2. 🔊 _____   3. 🔊 _____

4. 🔊 _____   5. 🔊 _____   6. 🔊 _____

7. 🔊 _____   8. 🔊 _____   9. 🔊 _____

10. 🔊 _____   11. 🔊 _____   12. 🔊 _____

13. 🔊 _____   14. 🔊 _____   15. 🔊 _____

B. Polysyllables（12 points） 多音节

1. 🔊 _____   2. 🔊 _____   3. 🔊 _____

4. 🔊 _____

汉语拼音入门　练习册

Introduction to Standard Chinese *Pinyin* System
Workbook

6

Name : _____

Class : _____ Year : _____

📖 Warm-up

Please listen to the recording for a review of the compound vowels learned in class.

热身活动：请听录音，复习课上所学的复元音韵母。

Compound Vowels 复元音韵母

1	2	3	4
ai	ei	ao	ou
爱（ài）	杯（bēi）	袄（ǎo）	鸥（ōu）
love	cup	Chinese-style coat	gull

5	6	7	8	9
ia	ie	ua	uo	üe
鸭（yā）	叶（yè）	蛙（wā）	蜗（wō）	月（yuè）
duck	leaf	frog	snail	moon

Part 1

Please listen to the recording and draw a line to link each picture with its corresponding compound vowel. （9 points）

请听录音，将图片与相对应的韵母用线连起来。

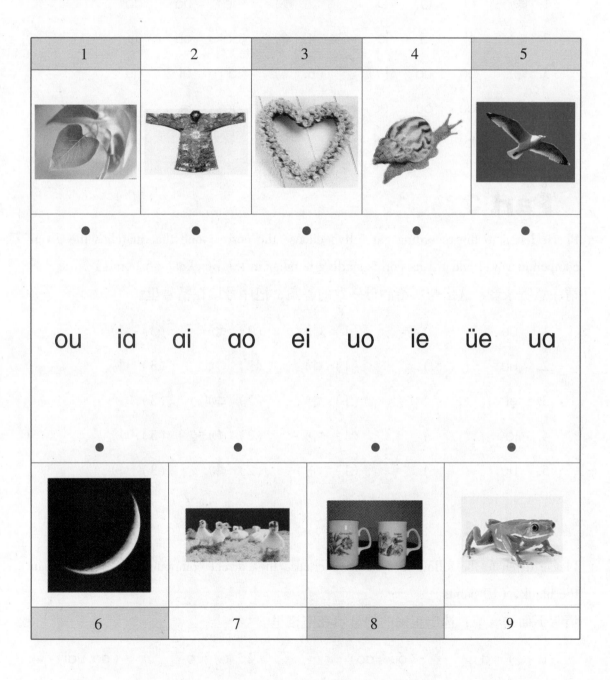

ou   ia   ai   ao   ei   uo   ie   üe   ua

Part 2

Circle the compound vowel you hear. (9 points)

圈出所听到的韵母。

1. 🔊 ai　ia　ei　　　2. 🔊 üe　uo　ao

3. 🔊 ei　ai　ie　　　4. 🔊 uo　ou　üe

5. 🔊 uo　ua　ia　　　6. 🔊 ia　ai　au

7. 🔊 ao　ou　uo　　　8. 🔊 üe　ie　ua

9. 🔊 ie　ia　ei

Part 3

Please listen to the recording carefully, choose the correct one that matches the given compound vowel and fill its corresponding number in the bracket. (5 points)

请注意听录音，选出与所给韵母一致的答案，把序号填在括号里。

1. üe　(　　)　　　(1) 🔊　　(2) 🔊　　(3) 🔊

2. uo　(　　)　　　(1) 🔊　　(2) 🔊　　(3) 🔊

3. ei　(　　)　　　(1) 🔊　　(2) 🔊　　(3) 🔊

4. ia　(　　)　　　(1) 🔊　　(2) 🔊　　(3) 🔊

5. ua　(　　)　　　(1) 🔊　　(2) 🔊　　(3) 🔊

Part 4

Please listen to the following syllables, choose the correct compound vowel and fill in the blank. (10 points)

请听下面的音节，选出正确的韵母填在空格里。

1. 🔊 d＿＿＿　(ou ao)　　　2. 🔊 c＿＿＿　(ao ai)

3. 🔊 g＿＿＿　(ou ao)　　　4. 🔊 b＿＿＿　(ei ai)

5. 🔊　x ＿＿＿＿　　（üe　ie ）　　6. 🔊　j ＿＿＿＿　　（uɑ　iɑ ）

7. 🔊　z ＿＿＿＿　　（uo　uɑ）　　8. 🔊　h ＿＿＿＿　　（uɑ　iɑ ）

9. 🔊　b ＿＿＿＿　　（ei　ie ）　　10. 🔊　sh ＿＿＿＿　　（ou　uo）

▶ Part 5

Please listen to the recording carefully and find the missing compound vowel for each syllable. （15 points）

请注意听录音，为每一个音节找到相对应的韵母。

1. 🔊　l ＿＿＿＿＿＿＿　●　　　　●　ɑi

2. 🔊　t ＿＿＿＿＿＿＿　●　　　　●　ei

3. 🔊　q ＿＿＿＿＿＿＿　●　　　　●　ɑo

4. 🔊　p ＿＿＿＿＿＿＿　●　　　　●　ou

5. 🔊　x ＿＿＿＿＿＿＿　●　　　　●　iɑ

6. 🔊　m ＿＿＿＿＿＿＿　●　　　　●　ie

7. 🔊　zh ＿＿＿＿＿＿＿　●　　　　●　uɑ

8. 🔊　n ＿＿＿＿＿＿＿　●　　　　●　uo

9. 🔊　p ＿＿＿＿＿＿＿　●　　　　●　üe

10. 🔊　g ＿＿＿＿＿＿＿　●

11. 🔊　k ＿＿＿＿＿＿＿　●

12. 🔊　j ＿＿＿＿＿＿＿　●

13. 🔊　zh ＿＿＿＿＿＿＿　●

14. 🔊　sh ＿＿＿＿＿＿＿　●

15. 🔊　k ＿＿＿＿＿＿＿　●

Part 6

Please listen to the following syllables and write out the missing compound vowel with its tone mark. （10 points）

请听下面的音节，一一写出韵母并标上声调。

1. 🔊 m ___   2. 🔊 g ___   3. 🔊 x ___   4. 🔊 h ___   5. 🔊 j ___

6. 🔊 zh ___   7. 🔊 j ___   8. 🔊 r ___   9. 🔊 d ___   10. 🔊 z ___

Part 7

Please listen to the recording and write down the syllable with its tone mark according to what you hear. （42 points）

请听录音，写出所听到的音节并标上声调。

A. Monosyllables （30 points）　单音节

1. 🔊 _____   2. 🔊 _____   3. 🔊 _____

4. 🔊 _____   5. 🔊 _____   6. 🔊 _____

7. 🔊 _____   8. 🔊 _____   9. 🔊 _____

10. 🔊 _____   11. 🔊 _____   12. 🔊 _____

13. 🔊 _____   14. 🔊 _____   15. 🔊 _____

B. Polysyllables （12 points）　多音节

1. 🔊 _____   2. 🔊 _____   3. 🔊 _____

4. 🔊 _____   5. 🔊 _____   6. 🔊 _____

汉语拼音入门　练习册

Introduction to Standard Chinese *Pinyin* System
Workbook

7

Name : _____

Class : _____ Year： _____

🔊 Warm-up

Please listen to the recording for a review of the compound vowels learned in class.

热身活动：请听录音，复习课上所学的复元音韵母。

Compound Vowels 复元音韵母			
1	2	3	4
iao	iou (iu)	uai	uei (ui)
药（yào）	油（yóu）	外（wài）	喂（wèi）
medicine	oil	outside	Hello（on the phone）

Part 1

Please listen to the recording and draw a line to link each picture with its corresponding compound vowel. （4 points）

请听录音，将图片与相对应的韵母用线连起来。

1	2	3	4
●	●	●	●
●	●	●	●
iou（iu）	uei（ui）	iao	uai

Part 2

Circle the compound vowel you hear. （5 points）

圈出所听到的韵母。

1. 🔊　　iu　　uai　　ui

2. 🔊　　iao　　ui　　uai

3. 🔊　　uai　　iao　　ui

4. 🔊　　iu　　ui　　iao

5. 🔊　　uai　　ui　　iu

Part 3

Please listen to the recording carefully, choose the correct one that matches the given compound vowel and fill its corresponding number in the bracket. （4 points）

每道题有三个选项，请注意听录音，选出与所给韵母一致的答案，把序号填在括号里。

1. iu　　（　　）　　（1）🔊　　（2）🔊　　（3）🔊

2. ui　　（　　）　　（1）🔊　　（2）🔊　　（3）🔊

3. iao　　（　　）　　（1）🔊　　（2）🔊　　（3）🔊

4. uai　　（　　）　　（1）🔊　　（2）🔊　　（3）🔊

Part 4

Please listen to the following syllables, choose the correct compound vowel and fill in the blank. （9 points）

请听下面的音节，选出正确的韵母填在空格里。

1. 🔊　m _____　　（iao　　iu）

2. 🔊　d _____　　（iu　　ui）

3. 🔊 zh _____　　　　（ uɑi　　 ui ）

4. 🔊 l _____　　　　（ iɑo　　 iu ）

5. 🔊 g _____　　　　（ ui　　 uɑi ）

6. 🔊 q _____　　　　（ iɑo　　 iu ）

7. 🔊 sh _____　　　　（ uɑi　　 ui ）

8. 🔊 x _____　　　　（ iu　　 iɑo ）

9. 🔊 ch _____　　　　（ uɑi　　 ui ）

▶Part 5

Please listen to the following syllables and write out the missing compound vowel with its tone mark. （10 points）

请听下面的音节，一一写出韵母并标上声调。

1. 🔊 p ____　 2. 🔊 d ____　 3. 🔊 t ____　 4. 🔊 n ____　 5. 🔊 l ____

6. 🔊 g ____　 7. 🔊 k ____　 8. 🔊 j ____　 9. 🔊 h ____　 10. 🔊 sh ____

▶Part 6

Please listen to the recording and write down the syllable with its tone mark according to what you hear. （68 points）

请听录音，写出所听到的音节并标上声调。

A. Monosyllables （38 points）　单音节

1. 🔊 _____　　　 2. 🔊 _____　　　 3. 🔊 _____

4. 🔊 _____　　　 5. 🔊 _____　　　 6. 🔊 _____

7. 🔊 _____　　　 8. 🔊 _____　　　 9. 🔊 _____

10. 🔊 _____　　 11. 🔊 _____　　 12. 🔊 _____

13. 🔊 _____　　 14. 🔊 _____　　 15. 🔊 _____

16. 🔊 _____   17. 🔊 _____   18. 🔊 _____

19. 🔊 _____

B．Polysyllables（30 points）　多音节

1. 🔊 _____   2. 🔊 _____

3. 🔊 _____   4. 🔊 _____

5. 🔊 _____   6. 🔊 _____

7. 🔊 _____   8. 🔊 _____

9. 🔊 _____   10. 🔊 _____

汉语拼音入门   练习册

Introduction to Standard Chinese *Pinyin* System

Workbook

8

Name : _____

Class : _____   Year: _____

▲Warm-up

Please listen to the recording for a review of the front nasal simple or compound vowels learned in class.

热身活动：请听录音，复习课上所学的前鼻韵母。

Front Nasal Simple or Compound Vowels 前鼻韵母

1	2	3	4
an	en	in	ün
岸（àn）	摁（èn）	印（yìn）	云（yún）
shore	press with fingers/ hands	stamp	cloud

5	6	7	8
ian	uan	üan	uen（un）
烟（yān）	碗（wǎn）	圆（yuán）	蚊（wén）
smoke/cigaret	bowl	circle	mosquito

Part 1

Please listen to the recording and draw a line to link each picture with its corresponding front nasal simple or compound vowel. (8 points)

请听录音，将图片与相对应的韵母用线连起来。

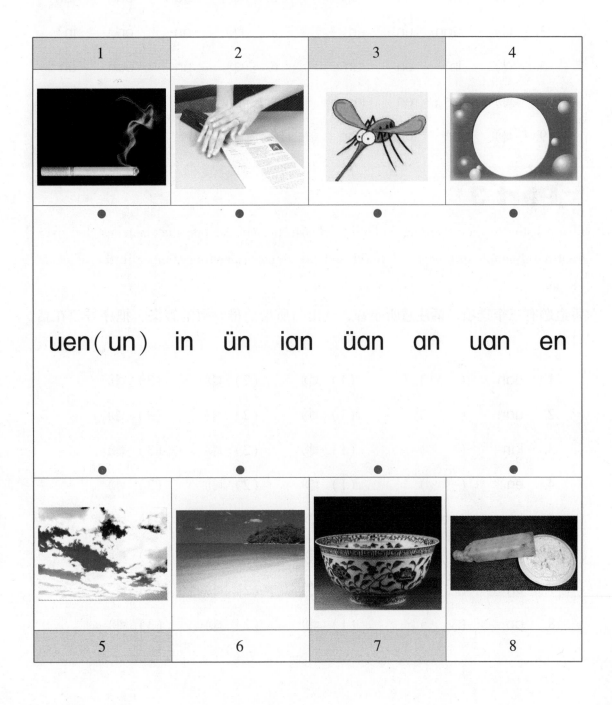

▶Part 2

Circle the front nasal simple or compound vowel you hear.（10 points）

圈出所听到的韵母。

1. 🔊 en   un   ün   2. 🔊 üan   uan   ian

3. 🔊 uan   un   en   4. 🔊 an   en   in

5. 🔊 in   en   ian   6. 🔊 un   üan   ün

7. 🔊 an   en   in   8. 🔊 un   en   an

9. 🔊 an   uan   üan   10. 🔊 in   en   ün

▶Part 3

Please listen to the recording carefully, choose the correct one that matches the given front nasal simple or compound vowel and fill its corresponding number in the bracket. （8 points）

每道题有三个选项，请注意听录音，选出与所给韵母一致的答案，把序号填在括号里。

1. üan   （   ）   (1) 🔊   (2) 🔊   (3) 🔊

2. uan   （   ）   (1) 🔊   (2) 🔊   (3) 🔊

3. ian   （   ）   (1) 🔊   (2) 🔊   (3) 🔊

4. en   （   ）   (1) 🔊   (2) 🔊   (3) 🔊

5. in   （   ）   (1) 🔊   (2) 🔊   (3) 🔊

6. un   （   ）   (1) 🔊   (2) 🔊   (3) 🔊

7. ün   （   ）   (1) 🔊   (2) 🔊   (3) 🔊

8. an   （   ）   (1) 🔊   (2) 🔊   (3) 🔊

Part 4

Please listen to the following syllables, choose the correct front nasal simple or compound vowel and fill in the blank. (10 points)

请听下面的音节，选出正确的韵母填在空格里。

1. 🔊 s ____ (an   en)   2. 🔊 j ____ (ün   in)

3. 🔊 m ____ (en   in)   4. 🔊 h ____ (un   uan)

5. 🔊 q ____ (an   ian)   6. 🔊 x ____ (üan   ian)

7. 🔊 j ____ (ün   üan)   8. 🔊 d ____ (un   uan)

9. 🔊 zh ____ (an   en)   10. 🔊 s ____ (uan   un)

Part 5

Please listen to the recording and find the missing front nasal simple or compound vowel for each syllable. (15 points)

请注意听录音，为每一个音节找到相对应的前鼻韵母。

1. 🔊 l _____ •   • an
2. 🔊 t _____ •   • en
3. 🔊 q _____ •   • in
4. 🔊 p _____ •   • ün
5. 🔊 x _____ •   • ian
6. 🔊 m _____ •   • uan
7. 🔊 zh _____ •   • üan
8. 🔊 n _____ •   • un
9. 🔊 j _____ •
10. 🔊 ch _____ •
11. 🔊 k _____ •
12. 🔊 d _____ •
13. 🔊 zh _____ •
14. 🔊 sh _____ •
15. 🔊 g _____ •

Part 6

Please listen to the following syllables and write out the missing front nasal simple or compound vowel with its tone mark. （10 points）

请听下面的音节，一一写出韵母并标上声调。

1. 🔊 f____　2. 🔊 q ____　3. 🔊 zh ____　4. 🔊 m ____　5. 🔊 j____

6. 🔊 n ____　7. 🔊 g ____　8. 🔊 t ____　9. 🔊 h ____　10. 🔊 ch ____

Part 7

Please listen to the recording and write down the syllable with its tone mark according to what you hear. （39 points）

请听录音，写出所听到的音节并标上声调。

A. Monosyllables （9 points）　单音节

1. 🔊 _____　　2. 🔊 _____　　3. 🔊 _____

4. 🔊 _____　　5. 🔊 _____　　6. 🔊 _____

7. 🔊 _____　　8. 🔊 _____　　9. 🔊 _____

B. Polysyllables （30 points）　多音节

1. 🔊 _____　　2. 🔊 _____

3. 🔊 _____　　4. 🔊 _____

5. 🔊 _____　　6. 🔊 _____

7. 🔊 _____　　8. 🔊 _____

9. 🔊 _____　　10. 🔊 _____

汉语拼音入门　练习册

Introduction to Standard Chinese *Pinyin* System
Workbook

9

Name : _____

Class : _____ Year : _____

📖 Warm-up

Please listen to the recording for a review of the back nasal simple or compound vowels learned in class.

热身活动：请听录音，复习课上所学的后鼻韵母。

Back Nasal Simple or Compound Vowels 后鼻韵母

1	2	3	4
ang	eng	ing	ong
昂（áng）	灯（dēng）	鹰（yīng）	钟（zhōng）
to hold one's head high	lamp	hawk	clock

5	6	7	8
iang	uang	iong	ueng
羊（yáng）	网（wǎng）	泳（yǒng）	翁（wēng）
sheep	net	to swim	old man

▎Part 1

Please listen to the recording and draw a line to link each picture with its corresponding back nasal simple or compound vowel. (8 points)

请听录音，将图片与相对应的韵母用线连起来。

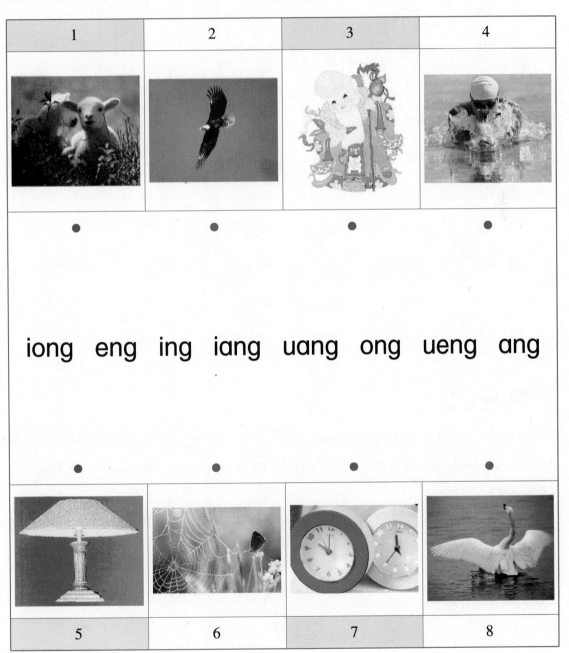

▶Part 2

Circle the back nasal simple or compound vowel you hear. （10 points）

圈出所听到的韵母。

1. 🔊　　ueng　　　ong　　　iong

2. 🔊　　iang　　　ang　　　uang

3. 🔊　　ing　　　iang　　　ang

4. 🔊　　ing　　　ong　　　iong

5. 🔊　　ing　　　ang　　　eng

6. 🔊　　eng　　　ong　　　ing

7. 🔊　　eng　　　ong　　　iong

8. 🔊　　uang　　　eng　　　ang

9. 🔊　　ong　　　ang　　　ueng

10. 🔊　　iong　　　ing　　　iang

▶Part 3

Please listen to the recording carefully，choose the correct one that matches the given back nasal simple or compound vowel and fill its corresponding number in the bracket. （8 points）

每道题有三个选项，请注意听录音，选出与所给韵母一致的答案，把序号填在括号里。

1. eng　　（　　）　　　（1）🔊　　　（2）🔊　　　（3）🔊

2. ing　　（　　）　　　（1）🔊　　　（2）🔊　　　（3）🔊

3. ang　　（　　）　　　（1）🔊　　　（2）🔊　　　（3）🔊

4. ong　　（　　）　　　（1）🔊　　　（2）🔊　　　（3）🔊

5. iang   (   )   (1) 🔊   (2) 🔊   (3) 🔊

6. uang   (   )   (1) 🔊   (2) 🔊   (3) 🔊

7. iong   (   )   (1) 🔊   (2) 🔊   (3) 🔊

8. ueng   (   )   (1) 🔊   (2) 🔊   (3) 🔊

▶ Part 4

Please listen to the recording and find the missing back nasal simple or compound vowel
for each syllable. (15 points)

请注意听录音，为每一个音节找到相对应的韵母。

1. 🔊   t _____   •   • ang

2. 🔊   g _____   •   • eng

3. 🔊   q _____   •   • ing

4. 🔊   p _____   •   • ong

5. 🔊   x _____   •   • iang

6. 🔊   b _____   •   • uang

7. 🔊   zh _____   •   • iong

8. 🔊   r _____   •   • ueng

9. 🔊   j _____   •

10. 🔊   ch _____   •

11. 🔊   k _____   •

12. 🔊   d _____   •

13. 🔊   x _____   •

14. 🔊   sh _____   •

15. 🔊   w _____   •

Part 5

Please listen to the following syllables, choose the correct back nasal simple or compound vowel and fill in the blank. (10 points)

请听下面的音节，选出正确的韵母填在空格里。

1. ◁)) sh _____ （ang eng）　　2. ◁)) b _____ （eng ing）

3. ◁)) h _____ （ong ueng）　　4. ◁)) x _____ （iong iang）

5. ◁)) ch _____ （uang ang）　　6. ◁)) y _____ （ing ong）

7. ◁)) q _____ （ing iang）　　8. ◁)) zh _____ （ang eng）

9. ◁)) c _____ （ong ang）　　10. ◁)) z _____ （ang ong）

Part 6

Please listen to the following syllables and write out the missing back nasal simple or compound vowel with its tone mark. (10 points)

请听下面的音节，一一写出韵母并标上声调。

1. ◁)) j ___　2. ◁)) p ___　3. ◁)) zh ___　4. ◁)) f ___　5. ◁)) k ___

6. ◁)) q ___　7. ◁)) l ___　8. ◁)) g ___　9. ◁)) x ___　10. ◁)) c ___

Part 7

Please listen to the recording and write down the syllable with its tone mark according to what you hear. (39 points)

请听录音，写出所听到的音节并标上声调。

A. Monosyllables (9 points)　单音节

1. ◁)) _____　　2. ◁)) _____　　3. ◁)) _____

4. ◁)) _____　　5. ◁)) _____　　6. ◁)) _____

7. ◁)) _____　　8. ◁)) _____　　9. ◁)) _____

B. Polysyllables（30 points） 多音节

1. 🔊 _____

2. 🔊 _____

3. 🔊 _____

4. 🔊 _____

5. 🔊 _____

6. 🔊 _____

7. 🔊 _____

8. 🔊 _____

9. 🔊 _____

10. 🔊 _____

āéū
aoiu

汉语拼音入门　练习册

Introduction to Standard Chinese *Pinyin* System

Workbook

10

Name : _____

Class : _____ Year: _____

📕 **Warm-up**

Please listen to the recording for a review of the rules of Chinese syllables learned in class.

热身活动：请听录音，复习课上所学的汉语音节规则。

A. Rules for Syllable Separation　音节分隔规则

1	2	3	4
iā→yā	ū→wū	ǘ→yú	xǐài
鸭	屋	鱼	喜爱
duck	house	fish	to like

B. Rules for Omission　省略规则

1	2	3
j ü ān→juān	q ü ān→quān	x ü ǎn→xuǎn
捐	圈	选
to donate	circle	to choose

C. Rules for Marking Tones   声调标调规则

1	2	3	4	5
tiào	yǒu	hēi	liù	yuè
跳	友	黑	六	月
to jump	friend	black	six	moon

D. Rules for Spelling Disyllables and Polysyllables   双音节和多音节拼写规则

1	2
lǎoshī	Zhōngguó
老师	中国
teacher	China

E. Rules for Tone Sandhi   变调规则

1	2
bàba	jǔ qǐ shǒu
爸爸	举起手
dad	to raise one's hand

Part 1

Circle the syllable you hear. （10 points）

圈出所听到的音节。

1. 🔊 yā　　jiā　　yē
2. 🔊 suǒ　　wǒ　　huǒ
3. 🔊 chuáng　　wáng　　huáng
4. 🔊 juè　　què　　yuè
5. 🔊 yán　　qián　　yáng
6. 🔊 wáng　　wán　　huán
7. 🔊 lǚ　　nǚ　　xǔ
8. 🔊 jú　　yú　　yún
9. 🔊 lǜ　　qù　　yù
10. 🔊 yǒu　　liǔ　　jiǔ

Part 2

Please listen to the recording carefully, choose the corresponding *Pinyin* from the right frame and fill in the blank. （10 points）

请听录音，在右边框中选择与之相对应的拼音填在空格里。

1. 🔊 _____
2. 🔊 _____
3. 🔊 _____
4. 🔊 _____
5. 🔊 _____
6. 🔊 _____
7. 🔊 _____
8. 🔊 _____
9. 🔊 _____
10. 🔊 _____

wǔ	yào	wèi
yuǎn	yīng	yǔ
wén	yī	shí'èr　Xī'ān

▶Part 3

Please listen to the following syllables and write out the missing initial consonant. (5 points)
请听下面的音节，并一一写出声母。

1. ◀)) ____ ě   2. ◀)) ____ èn   3. ◀)) ____ ún   4. ◀)) ____ ài   5. ◀)) ____ īn

▶Part 4

Please listen to the recording and add tone marks to the following syllables. （20 points）
请听录音，为下面的音节标上声调。

A. Monosyllables （10 points） 单音节

1. ◀)) hao   2. ◀)) bai   3. ◀)) cuo   4. ◀)) xiong   5. ◀)) dei

6. ◀)) hua   7. ◀)) qiu   8. ◀)) dian   9. ◀)) gui   10. ◀)) dou

11. ◀)) kuai   12. ◀)) liang   13. ◀)) mei   14. ◀)) xia   15. ◀)) jue

16. ◀)) huang 17. ◀)) jie   18. ◀)) hou   19. ◀)) zhuan   20. ◀)) jiao

B. Polysyllables （10 points） 多音节

1. ◀)) gege   2. ◀)) meimei

3. ◀)) benzi   4. ◀)) nide

5. ◀)) juede   6. ◀)) xiexie

7. ◀)) mingzi   8. ◀)) yisi

9. ◀)) dongle   10. ◀)) xiansheng

Part 5

Please listen to the following disyllables or polysyllables and circle the correct one that conforms to the real pronunciation. （10 points）

请听下面的双音节或多音节，圈出与实际读音相符的一个。

	Chinese characters	English translation	*Pinyin*	Should be read as…	
1.	你好	hello	nǐ hǎo	（1） 🔊	（2） 🔊
2.	好久	a long time	hǎo jiǔ	（1） 🔊	（2） 🔊
3.	可口	tasty	kěkǒu	（1） 🔊	（2） 🔊
4.	所以	therefore；so	suǒyǐ	（1） 🔊	（2） 🔊
5.	洗澡	to take a bath	xǐzǎo	（1） 🔊	（2） 🔊
6.	李友	Li You	Lǐ Yǒu	（1） 🔊	（2） 🔊
7.	水果	fruit	shuǐguǒ	（1） 🔊	（2） 🔊
8.	只有	only	zhǐ yǒu	（1） 🔊	（2） 🔊
9.	举起手	to raise one's hand（s）	jǔ qǐ shǒu	（1） 🔊	（2） 🔊
10.	看一看	to take a look	kàn yī kàn	（1） 🔊	（2） 🔊

Part 6

Add the correct tone mark on the word "不"（bù）in the following words. （5 points）

给下面音节中的"不"（bù）加上实际读音的声调。

1. bu shì　　2. bu yào　　3. bu dǒng　　4. bucuò　　5. bu néng

Part 7

Add the correct tone mark on the word "一"（yī）in the following words. （5 points）

给下面音节中的"一"（yī）加上实际读音的声调。

1. yi bēi　　2. yiyàng　　3. yi gè　　4. yizhí　　5. yi diǎn

▶ Part 8

Please listen to the recording and write down the syllable with its tone mark according to what you hear. （35 points）

请听录音，写出所听到的音节并标上声调。

A. Monosyllables （15 points）　单音节

1. 🔊 _____　　　2. 🔊 _____　　　3. 🔊 _____

4. 🔊 _____　　　5. 🔊 _____　　　6. 🔊 _____

7. 🔊 _____　　　8. 🔊 _____　　　9. 🔊 _____

10. 🔊 _____　　11. 🔊 _____　　12. 🔊 _____

13. 🔊 _____　　14. 🔊 _____　　15. 🔊 _____

B. Polysyllables （20 points）　多音节

1. 🔊 _____　　　2. 🔊 _____　　　3. 🔊 _____

4. 🔊 _____　　　5. 🔊 _____　　　6. 🔊 _____

7. 🔊 _____　　　8. 🔊 _____　　　9. 🔊 _____

10. 🔊 _____

aéü

Answer Key　答案

Lesson 2

Part 1

Simple vowels

1. e　2. i　3. ü　4. o　5. er　6. u　7. a

Initial consonants

1. m　2. f　3. p　4. b

Part 2

1. a　2. ü　3. i　4. er　5. u　6. o　7. e　8. p　9. m　10. f

Part 3

1. (1)　2. (3)　3. (2)　4. (1)　5. (3)

Part 4

1. p　2. m　3. p　4. b　5. f

Part 5

1. m　2. b　3. f　4. p　5. p

Part 6

1. o　2. i　3. a　4. o　5. i　6. a　7. u　8. i　9. o　10. a

Part 7

1. o　2. u　3. a　4. u　5. i　6. i　7. u　8. o　9. u　10. o

Part 8

1. fa　2. po　3. mi　4. bo　5. fo　6. pa

7. bi　8. mo　9. bu　10. mu　11. ba　12. fu

13. pu　14. ma　15. pi　16. me　17. ba

Lesson 3

Part 1

    1. k   2. x   3. t   4. n   5. q   6. g   7. j   8. d   9. l   10. h

Part 2

    1. t   2. n   3. g   4. h   5. j   6. d   7. l   8. k   9. q   10. x

Part 3

    1. (2)   2. (1)   3. (3)   4. (2)   5. (3)

Part 4

    1. (1)   2. (3)   3. (2)   4. (1)   5. (2)

Part 5

    1. t   2. n   3. k   4. q   5. x   6. x   7. j   8. g   9. n   10. d

Part 6

    1. d   2. t   3. g   4. j   5. t   6. g   7. n   8. l   9. n   10. x

Part 7

    1. ne   2. gu   3. la   4. ku   5. da

    6. ji   7. ha   8. qu   9. de   10. na

    11. hu   12. xu   13. di   14. ta   15. ni

    16. ga   17. xi   18. du   19. te   20. nu

    21. ge   22. qi   23. he   24. li   25. nü

Lesson 4

Part 1

1. sh   2. zh   3. z   4. r   5. ch   6. s   7. c

Part 2

1. z   2. r   3. zh   4. c   5. sh   6. ch   7. s   8. c   9. z   10. sh

Part 3

1. (3)   2. (1)   3. (2)   4. (2)   5. (3)

Part 4

1. (2)   2. (1)   3. (3)   4. (1)   5. (2)

Part 5

1. c   2. sh   3. ch   4. s   5. c   6. ch   7. r   8. zh   9. r   10. s

Part 6

1. zh   2. z   3. ch   4. ch   5. z   6. sh   7. zh

Part 7

1. zi	2. zhu	3. cha	4. shi	5. re	6. si	7. ri
8. chu	9. zu	10. ru	11. su	12. ca	13. zhe	14. chi
15. she	16. chu	17. zha	18. zhi	19. sa	20. shu	21. cu
22. se	23. ci					

Lesson 5

Part 1

1. má   2. mǎ   3. mà   4. mā

Part 2

1. gē   2. dà   3. chú   4. nà   5. shì

6. qǐ   7. kě   8. lí   9. fū   10. yú

Part 3

1. （3）   2. （2）   3. （2）   4. （1）   5. （3）

Part 4

1. （2）   2. （3）   3. （1）   4. （2）   5. （1）

Part 5

1. （ˋ）   2. （－）   3. （ˊ）   4. （ˋ）   5. （ˇ）

6. （－）   7. （ˇ）   8. （ˊ）   9. （ˋ）

Part 6

1. lǐ   2. bà   3. pǔ   4. è   5. sǐ

6. de   7. sǎ   8. lǜ   9. ne   10. tú

Part 7

A

1. rì   2. bà   3. zhè   4. bù   5. dé

6. fā   7. jǐ   8. hé   9. kè   10. kù

11. lái   12. qù   13. lù   14. sì   15. nǐ

B

1. chúle   2. lǜshī   3. kělè   4. fùxí

Lesson 6

Part 1

  1. ie   2. ao   3. ai   4. uo   5. ou   6. üe   7. ia   8. ei   9. ua

Part 2

  1. ai   2. ao   3. ei   4. ou   5. ua   6. ia   7. uo   8. üe   9. ie

Part 3

  1. (3)   2. (1)   3. (3)   4. (2)   5. (2)

Part 4

  1. ou   2. ai   3. ao   4. ei   5. üe

  6. ia   7. uo   8. ua   9. ie   10. uo

Part 5

  1. ao   2. ou   3. ie   4. ai   5. üe   6. ao   7. ua   8. ie   9. ei

  10. uo   11. ai   12. ia   13. ai   14. ao   15. ou

Part 6

  1. m<u>ǎi</u>   2. g<u>ěi</u>   3. xi<u>à</u>   4. hu<u>ā</u>   5. ju<u>é</u>

  6. zh<u>ào</u>   7. ji<u>ě</u>   8. r<u>òu</u>   9. du<u>ō</u>   10. z<u>ài</u>

Part 7

  A

  1. cài   2. cháo   3. gāo   4. qiě   5. hǎo   6. huò   7. kāi   8. zhōu

  9. guò 10. zǒu   11. xiě   12. jiá   13. tài   14. shéi 15. děi

  B

  1. nüèdài   2. hòulái   3. kāfēi   4. jièshào   5. shòujià   6. shuōhuà

Lesson 7

Part 1

    1. uai   2. iao   3. iu   4. ui

Part 2

    1. ui   2. uai   3. iao   4. iu   5. uai

Part 3

    1.（1）   2.（3）   3.（2）   4.（3）

Part 4

    1. iao 2. iu 3. ui 4. iao 5. ui 6. iao 7. uai 8. iu 9. ui

Part 5

    1. p<u>iào</u>   2. d<u>uì</u>   3. t<u>uǐ</u>   4. n<u>iǎo</u>   5. l<u>iù</u>

    6. g<u>uài</u>   7. k<u>uài</u>   8. j<u>iāo</u>   9. h<u>uí</u>   10. sh<u>uài</u>

Part 6

    A

    1. tiáo   2. niú   3. liào   4. kuī   5. huài

    6. jiào   7. jiù   8. qiāo   9. tuī   10. cuī

    11. suī   12. piào   13. shuǐ 14. chuī   15. ruì

    16. qiú   17. miù   18. diāo   19. diū

    B

    1. píjiǔ   2. jiàoshì   3. shuìjiào   4. dàxiǎo   5. huíjiā

    6. kāihuì   7. qíguài   8. zuìhòu   9. kuàilè   10. dǎqiú

Lesson 8

Part 1

1. ian   2. en   3. un   4. üan   5. ün   6. an   7. uan   8. in

Part 2

1. un   2. ian   3. uan   4. in   5. en

6. üan   7. an   8. un   9. üan   10. ün

Part 3

1. （1）   2. （2）   3. （2）   4. （1）

5. （3）   6. （3）   7. （2）   8. （3）

Part 4

1. an   2. in   3. en   4. uan   5. ian

6. üan   7. ün   8. un   9. en   10. uan

Part 5

1. in   2. ian   3. üan   4. an   5. in   6. en   7. uan   8. ian

9. ün   10. an   11. un   12. uan   13. uan   14. en   15. an

Part 6

1. f<u>àn</u>   2. qu<u>àn</u>   3. zh<u>ǔn</u>   4. m<u>iàn</u>   5. j<u>ùn</u>

6. n<u>ín</u>   7. g<u>ēn</u>   8. t<u>iān</u>   9. h<u>uān</u>   10. ch<u>ūn</u>

Part 7

A

1. chuán   2. rén   3. duǎn   4. biàn   5. xuǎn

6. xīn   7. lán   8. qún   9. sūn

B

1. jīntiān   2. jūnrén   3. nánguān   4. juānqián   5. búdàn

6. chēzhàn   7. chènshān   8. chūntiān   9. diànhuà   10. quánqín

Lesson 9

Part 1

1. iang   2. ing   3. ueng   4. iong   5. eng   6. uang   7. ong   8. ang

Part 2

1. ueng   2. uang   3. iang   4. iong   5. ing

6. eng   7. ong   8. ang   9. ueng   10. ing

Part 3

1. （1）   2. （3）   3. （3）   4. （2）

5. （2）   6. （1）   7. （2）   8. （3）

Part 4

1. ing   2. ong   3. iang   4. ang   5. ing

6. eng   7. uang   8. eng   9. iang   10. uang

11. ong   12. ang   13. iong   14. uang   15. ueng

Part 5

1. ang   2. ing   3. ong   4. iang   5. uang

6. ong   7. ing   8. ang   9. ong   10. ang

Part 6

1. jiǎng   2. péng   3. zhāng   4. fáng   5. kuàng

6. qǐng   7. lán   8. guāng   9. xióng   10. cóng

Part 7

A

1. tāng   2. néng   3. zhèng   4. chàng   5. hóng

6. liǎng   7. shēng   8. míng   9. chuáng

B

1. bāngmáng   2. gōngyǎng   3. sòngyáng   4. guāngróng   5. qiángzhuàng

6. Xiānggǎng   7. pīngpāng   8. dāngrán   9. bù dǒng   10. bàngōng

Lesson 10

Part 1

    1. yā   2. wǒ   3. wáng   4. yuè   5. yán

    6. wán   7. xǔ   8. jú   9. qù   10. yǒu

Part 2

    1. wén   2. yǔ   3. wǔ   4. yào   5. Xī'ān

    6. wèi   7. yīng   8. yuǎn   9. yī   10. shí'èr

Part 3

    1. y   2. w   3. y   4. w   5. y

Part 4

    A

    1. hǎo   2. bái   3. cuò   4. xióng   5. děi

    6. huā   7. qiú   8. diàn   9. guì   10. dōu

    11. kuài   12. liǎng   13. méi   14. xià   15. jué

    16. huáng   17. jiě   18. hòu   19. zhuān   20. jiào

    B

    1. gēge   2. mèimei   3. běnzi   4. nǐ de   5. juéde

    6. xièxie   7. míngzi   8. yìsi   9. dǒngle   10. xiānsheng

Part 5

    1. (2)   2. (1)   3. (2)   4. (2)   5. (1)

    6. (2)   7. (1)   8. (1)   9. (2)   10. (2)

Part 6

    1. bú shì   2. bú yào   3. bù dǒng   4. búcuò   5. bù néng

Part 7

    1. yì bēi   2. yíyàng   3. yí gè   4. yìzhí   5. yì diǎn

Part 8

A

1. yī	2. qù	3. xuān	4. yě	5. yòng
6. wǎn	7. yǒu	8. yǔ	9. jú	10. wǔ
11. yuǎn	12. yuē	13. wáng	14. juān	15. xú

B

1. yìsi	2. nǚ'ér	3. jiějie	4. wǒmen	5. xuésheng
6. yīnyuè	7. yīnwèi	8. juéde	9. děng yi děng	10. wàngle